Next Level Living

Today's Guide
for Tomorrow's
Abundant Life

Quantity discounts are available on bulk orders.
Contact info@TAGPublishers.com for more information.

TAG Publishing, LLC
2618 S. Lipscomb
Amarillo, TX 79109
www.TAGPublishers.com

Office (806) 373-0114
Fax (806) 373-4004
info@TAGPublishers.com

ISBN: 9781934606353

First Edition

Next Level Living

Today's Guide
for Tomorrow's
Abundant Life

Linda McLean

DEDICATION

I dedicate this book to my family: Your love and support lights my way as I continue to climb from level to level in life. Thank you for traveling with me on this incredible journey!

To my husband Scot: After 32 years you still stand beside me, always seeking new ways to support me. This book would not be possible without your partnership. My husband, my eternal "boyfriend," my best friend.

To my daughters Brittany and Paige: Words cannot express what joy you bring to my life. I love you as high as the sky and as deep, deep, deep as the sea!

ACKNOWLEDGEMENTS

Creating a list of all those who deserve acknowledgement for supporting me during the writing of Next Level Living has been more challenging than I ever imagined.

To try and acknowledge all the people in my life who have influenced, supported and guided me on the journey to writing my first book is an insurmountable task. Therefore, I would like to give a blanket thank you to all of you for being a part of my life, whether for just a season or if you have walked alongside me on my life path for many years.

And in no order of preference I thank the following...

My God, for being the rock that I cling to and the sunshine I lift my eyes up to, knowing that life is good and precious. For the Scripture in Philippians 4:13 says: "I can do all this through him who gives me strength."

The great women (you know who you are) at the beginning of this journey who asked me how to reach new levels in their lives, thus encouraging me to don my Next Level Living guide hat for the first time and teach the class that inspired this book.

Bob Proctor and Gina Hayden who gave me hope in times of despair, education to think differently and dedicated friendship beyond measure. Your words of wisdom resonate on many levels. Your constant belief that I have the power to continue to conquer more and more provides me with hope, drive and determination. Your insistence that I can change lives around the world propels me forward!

Dee Burks, Louisa Tremann and Christine Whitmarsh, my partners in this project who have worked tirelessly beside me to make this dream a reality. Thank you for fixing my errors, adding clarity to my thoughts, and giving my ideas the right words. Your unwavering belief in this book gave me everything I needed to cross the finish line. Words truly cannot express my deep appreciation.

Mark Walker, my business coach who I am also privileged to call my friend. Thank you for giving me guidance, nudging and support as I continue to test my new set of wings. You help me soar!

My clients who continue to entrust me with their personal and professional goals and guide them to higher levels. This in turn encourages me to always reach higher.

Patti Knoles for designing the cover art and illustrations that brought the concepts of Next Level Living to life.

Spicer Photography - Martha and Jeff for your critical eye and persistence to get just the rights shots and your help in selecting the best from the massive selection of photos.

Every project needs a firm foundation built on support and encouragement, especially when the going gets tough. Thank you to my dear family and friends who have blessed me with such a strong foundation.

And speaking of support…. hugs to all of my girlfriends: my relentless, lifelong cheerleaders!

Lastly, I'd like to thank you, the reader. It has been a labor of love to share these life changing processes for you to incorporate into your daily, weekly, monthly, and yearly life plans. I wish you all your heart desires and may your journey be filled with extreme success in all areas of your life. I openly invite you to share your suggestions for improvement and your experiences working with these processes. Your feedback is greatly appreciated and will definitely be a contributing factor to future books.

CONTENTS

Section Three ◆ SUPPORT YOUR JOURNEY WITH AFFIRMATIONS AND VISUALIZATION

Section Four ◆ CELEBRATE YOUR JOURNEY

FOREWORD

I have worked with and observed Linda McLean in action for at least 20 years, and I felt honored that she would ask me to write the foreword to her book, *Next Level Living: Today's Guide to Tomorrow's Abundant Life*. I've been involved in the self help industry for over 50 years, and when you study one thing for that long, you quickly begin to recognize what's real and what's not. Take my word for it: you have your hands on a jewel that's borne from years of practical experience.

Many years ago I heard Zig Ziglar say that if you help enough people get what they want, they'll give you what you want. Linda McLean has followed that philosophy for many years. As a result, she and her family live what many would consider a charmed life, but it's not by accident. It's because of the truth based in Ziglar's statement that she followed to the letter. I've never known anyone who can create order out of chaos as well as she does. She has the unique ability to help individuals do the type of personal planning that helps them move forward no matter the challenges they are facing. Linda has also helped numerous businesses take confusion and transform it into a smooth running operation that maximizes profit, turns work into fun and leaves the business operator and their clients in a very happy and prosperous state.

Next Level Living is an incredible guide that offers sage advice, practical wisdom, and intelligently directed action all in one book. "Day 1 – Decide to Do Something" is so simple, yet so powerful. Nothing happens until you make a decision. Many people live in paralysis with their dreams in their head, because they never make a decision to step out and act. They spend all of their time thinking about what to do, planning and waiting until they're ready. Consider this:

even if you step out and make the wrong move, you can always change it and will probably have learned a valuable lesson in the process.

"Day 2 – Study Gratitude" is another simple but extraordinary concept. Gratitude puts you in close connection with your source of supply. Wallace D. Wattles, in his book, *The Science of Getting Rich* wrote, "The whole process of mental adjustment and atonement can be summed up in one word: gratitude."

I guarantee, if a person were to act on these two things alone – stepping out and taking action on what they want and being grateful every day, their whole world would change so much they probably wouldn't recognize it in six month's time. If that's all you learned from this book, you would have recouped your investment one hundred fold!

If this foreword is sounding like a testimonial, that's probably because it is. I have personally recommended Linda McLean and her company to a number of clients in a number of different countries and every time I do, I am absolutely certain that the client will win. I am equally as confident in recommending this book. I know that if you follow what is laid out in Next Level Living, you will also win.

Enjoy the journey.

Bob Proctor
Teacher in The Secret,
bestselling author of *You Were Born Rich*

INTRODUCTION
THE JOURNEY BEGINS...

Many people look at my life now thinking it's so charmed and easy. What many don't see is how I reached a higher level of business success and personal happiness by overcoming many obstacles in my life. Obstacles some of you may have experienced as well: deep guilt over past decisions...feeling unworthy because of ill treatment by friends or family...staring heartbroken at a wedding dress and a suddenly cancelled wedding... career failures... marital challenges...

I overcame all of these challenges and more during my journey to Next Level Living. One of my greatest challenges was facing my own death. It's a story I'd like to share with you now.

Several years ago I was young, energetic, and my family was growing and doing well. It never even crossed my mind that I could have a health issue lurking behind the scenes. I guess we all think we will always be healthy and never be faced with a disease. That's the kind of thing that happens to "other people."

It all came upon me pretty fast. Suddenly, I was the other person. We had recently moved from Canada to the U.S., and it was more stressful than I had realized. Juggling two young children (one going into 4th grade and the other into 8th), finishing construction on our home, decorating, establishing my business, supporting my husband in the new role in his company, managing paperwork with a move from one country to another, among other responsibilities. Piling on top of all this was the emotional strain from leaving family, our church group, and friends. Starting fresh in so many aspects drowned me in stress. But of course, I didn't fully understand the effects until much later.

Within the first 60 days of arriving in the U.S., I decided to get my initial doctor's appointments scheduled. My first mammogram in a routine checkup showed a small imperfection. Next thing I knew, they were doing a biopsy. I was still positive that it was just part of the U.S. medical procedures and not that big of a deal, until the day I received a phone call saying the lump was malignant. I sat down in disbelief. How could this be happening to me?

My mother had experienced breast cancer and had a mastectomy at the age of 59. Nine years later, at the age of 68, she passed away with a reoccurrence of cancer. Brittany (our first child) was only 26 days old. I was devastated. It was very difficult to begin understanding how I would cope and carry on.

So, when the doctor said to me, "Linda, I am very sorry to tell you the biopsy confirmed that the lump is cancerous, and we will move quickly to schedule your surgery." I was shocked. All I could think about was my family. In the midst of it all, I knew I had a decision to make about how I would react to this news. I knew I had to dig deep, to visualize myself healthy and rely on my faith. We had just met the pastor of our new church a month earlier, yet he and the church had quickly embraced us and became our local family. They provided us with more support than we could have imagined. But in spite of the support we had and the positive thinking I was exercising, I was not prepared for what happened next.

One beautiful sunny day the girls were at school, Scot was at work, and I had just finished some business coaching calls. All of a sudden an overpowering sadness and fear came over me like a big, dark blanket. I felt like it was smothering me.

Fear ripped at my heart when I thought of what I would miss watching my girls grow up, how I wanted to grow old with Scot, travel the world, enjoy grandchildren one day, spend time with friends and relatives – all the things you just take for granted will happen one day. Remembering the heartache I experienced after losing my parents and missing them, I thought about how my family would miss me if it was my time to leave this Earth.

The sobbing was uncontrollable. I truly didn't know who to reach out to, who could help me, or how they could console me. I felt hopeless, afraid and alone.

We were new in the neighborhood, and I couldn't just show up at my neighbor's front door sobbing uncontrollably. This fear and sadness held me captive for two days. I didn't share it with anyone as I wasn't certain how to explain it, and in some weird way I felt it was something I had to push through myself. It was like being in a turbulent storm, and I had to find my own way through it.

Exhaustion finally took over. I fell to my knees and prayed that if God wanted to take me, that we would be prepared; my next steps would be clear, and that I would be infused with strength.

From that moment on, the oddest thing occurred. I felt a peacefulness I couldn't quite explain. I believe I moved to another level in releasing my fear.

Although I felt calmer, my breakdown didn't necessarily make life any easier because we were still in that waiting period before my surgery.

Despite it all, I continued doing my best to think positive thoughts. I embraced each day with hopefulness and moved on with our new life in the U.S.

And when things got to be too much and I felt the darkness threatening again, I would bring myself mentally back to that incredible, albeit odd moment, when I felt myself ascending to another level, where my fear didn't exist. It was comforting to know such a level existed.

My surgery was in December of 2000 and was successful. It was followed by radiation treatments. It has now been more than a decade since my surgery, and I believe that the focus of moving forward with faith and perseverance helped me ascend to that next level in my life.

As I write this, I am looking around at my current level. I see my husband (and best friend) of 32 years, my two amazing daughters who continaully work toward their own dreams, our wonderful friends and our beautiful home. I embrace and enjoy travel to new countries, and I love my work with clients from around the world. Each year, I celebrate my setting and reaching new goals. My spiritual walk is stronger than ever since I learned to rely on my faith as the driver of my journey, and God as the center stone that I've built my life around. Life is good.

These blessings and more serve as a personal confirmation that the Next Level Living journey is real. Please keep in mind, as you embark on your own journey, that your "next level" will look completely different than mine. The moral of my story is, that I managed to summon the strength to move forward from what was once a state of fear to a new level of living – and so can you.

What is keeping you trapped in a state of fear, worry or doubt? What is keeping you from freeing yourself and moving up to your Next Level of Living? It could be perceived life failures, unfulfilled goals, personal hardships, your inner voice filling your mind with negative, pessimistic garbage, or all of the above.

These are the things that are keeping you weighted down. They are barriers to the incredible, limitless change that is buried deep inside you.

My life changing personal experience brought the message into focus, loud and clear. To attain the next level, we must dig deep to find what holds us back. And have the courage to face and fix what we find.

As a matter of fact, you may be reading this and not be in a traumatic life situation at all. Maybe this book has come to you because you feel you have a great life and want *more*!

No matter what your motivation for embarking on this journey, it all starts with the question - how did I get here? Almost without exception, we each ask ourselves this question at some point in our lives.

It may occur at one of the many crossroads we encounter such as graduation, marriage, birth, death, career change, or illness. These are the moments we tend to step back and evaluate who we are, how far we have come, and which direction we want to go.

Some of these life changing events are expected and longed for, such as graduation or marriage. Others catch us by surprise and can leave us feeling lost and broken wondering what's next. During these times, we are forced to consider the bigger questions of life and actively choose our path. This is good and necessary, but what about those times when nothing much is happening?

What about when the days are zinging by with incredible speed and nothing is really wrong, but it just seems like there could be something more? How do we move forward, when most of the time, we feel like we are simply going through the motions of life and stumbling around in the dark?

This book features a specific sequence of insights to help you discover how you arrived at your current level of living, lessons focused on how to break free and move to the next level, along with the tools and exercises designed to propel you forward. Together, they will serve as a day-to-day roadmap from where you are now to a place where you have the true freedom to explore the limitless potential of your life. Welcome to the journey I call Next Level Living.

Next Level Living

Picture a blindfolded man who has been trapped in a basement for his whole life and knows nothing of the world beyond it. He feels his way around blindly in the dark, hoping to make sense of his limited reality.

Over in the corner, there is a staircase that he has fallen over many times, that leads out of the basement into the light. But he doesn't know to climb the stairs, because the basement level is all he knows.

Now imagine that his blindfold is removed, but the lights are still out in the basement. He's still in the dark, trying to make sense of the shadowy corners surrounding him. He doesn't know how to flip the light switch on the wall right in front of him, because he has never seen light and therefore has no ability to turn it on.

Even without the blindfold, the man's basement level living is dark but familiar, limiting but comfortable to him. The thought of moving to another level of living never occurs to him because he doesn't know it exists.

How many of us either live or have lived like the man in the dark, simply because we aren't aware of other options? We lack the knowledge that there are other levels above where light, a life without limits and a better reality await.

Next Level Living is your flashlight, your blueprint of the basement and most importantly, your map up the staircase to a next level of reality that you might not know even exists.

It is a journey in personal transformation that has the power to change your perception of where you are in life, where you want to be and how to get there. It is the staircase that has been there waiting for you the whole time; but you never saw it there in the shadows.

We all deserve the chance to evolve and grow into a greater version of ourselves, exercising our personal potential to its fullest level. And the good news is, no matter how much we personally grow and evolve there is always a next level. No matter how much light appears to surround you right now, there is always another staircase waiting to bring you to that brand new level of living above.

Goals of the Journey

The information you will read in these pages is meant to be worked through, not just absorbed. I will challenge you to think about who you are and what you want. I will encourage you to set goals that stretch your ideas of what is possible, and I will hold you accountable to take action and set your plans in motion.

I will ask you to be honest with yourself and be as objective as possible in order to deal with "what is" in your life. You will examine the past and let go of the ideas, beliefs and issues that stand in your way.

This isn't meant to be an easy journey, it's meant to be a satisfying and fulfilling one, and at times that may be uncomfortable. Because, let's face it – change doesn't always feel good.

This is one of the reasons why the vast majority of people never come to terms with the life of possibilities they once imagined. They languish behind a wall of "should," "have to," and "can't," and impossibility that blinds them to the vast array of options that exist at all times all around them. This blindness, like the man in the basement with the blindfold, is no more common in women than in men, but there is a greater tendency among women to accept what we see as the "reality" of our situation and to not look assertively for other options.

Once we understand the infinite range of possibilities and how to access them, we will need only one tool to see where the solution lies within – the tool of BELIEF! If it was easy, anyone could do it. Perhaps that is the reason that so many people choose to accept "reality" and stop looking for the life they hope exists. It's as if we need to reach the point of being completely disillusioned, before we are willing to take the steps to change our situation. Once we reach that place, we are willing to do what is necessary instead of what is comfortable. It is the first step on the staircase.

I am not going to suggest that you change jobs, change scenery, or change partners to achieve Next Level Living. What is good in your life right now will not stand in the way of a better life. All I will do is suggest that you examine your life and uncover the real "you." The version of you with tremendous potential lurking beneath the surface; the "you" that used to dream of something more.

The you that laughed often, loved much, and reveled in the joy of living. There is a "you" that is fully you, and my job is to give you the tools to uncover that amazing person and show you how to get the fulfilling and happy life you deserve. Most of the time, the biggest change we need to make is in our thinking, not in our situation, although sometimes we need to face the facts about that situation and make some changes there as well.

Next Level Living is a reminder that you can change. This journey is your avenue for exploring the possibilities. As you embrace your power, we will celebrate the amazing, capable, brilliant, loving and confident person that you are.

Tools for the Journey

As you journey to your next level of living, there are several tools that will maximize your success. First, you will be writing a daily gratitude list. To help you with this you can use a companion Next Level Living Workbook that you can purchase where you found this book.

The workbook provides an organized place to record your daily gratitude list, do your daily written actions, and reflect on your accomplishments every day.

Each day's activities and instructions will be replicated and pre-formatted for you in the workbook, so all you'll need to do is fill in the blanks. Your workbook will serve as a guide, connecting the days of your journey with consistent messaging and a way of focusing wholly on your Next Level Living journey.

If, however, you choose not to purchase the companion workbook, please have a notebook available as you move through each section to complete the activities. And lastly, if you find yourself needing some additional support along the way, please let me know. There are Next Level webinars, teleseminars, telephone and in-person coaching sessions available to support you in your process of change and growth. Please visit (www. NextLevelLivingBook.com) for more information. I support you on your journey and am very excited for you success.

Jewels for the Journey

Like the jewels hidden on a treasure hunt, the Jewels of your Next Level Living journey can be found throughout the book and sometimes when you least expect them. These bonus gems of insight and calls to action are designed to enhance and accelerate your journey to the next level.

Map Your Next Level Journey

Each day's overall message and lessons include a sequence of activities to keep you moving in the direction of your next level. The aim is to balance knowledge and personal discovery, with active, mindful participation. After all, only reading about a journey doesn't get you anywhere.

Every day you will take a new step up by...

◆ Writing out a gratitude list

◆ Reading your Next Level Lesson

◆ Completing an Action Item related to the day's lesson

◆ Wrapping up each day with a time of reflection

I have created each day to take you no more than seven minutes in the morning and then another 15 minutes in the day including the reading, actions, and daily wrap up. If you knew 22 minutes a day for 32 days could change your life, would you be willing to invest that much time in yourself?

Many people I encounter underestimate what they are capable of. If you feel you just can't find 22 minutes out of every 24 hour day, you may be one of them. I encourage you to jump in and try the first 15 days, do your best, and see what happens. At that point you can assess if taking this journey is doable for you. Never underestimate what you can achieve in 32 days!

Engage in Change

I admire successful athletes, especially when I learn what it took to get where they are – their personal next level. I watch in awe and admiration the journey they embarked on to rise to the top of their game.

How many times, when you're watching a game, do you say or hear from others comments such as "he has a gift" or "she is lucky"? Top notch athletes have a way of making what they do look so effortless, that it's easy to forget the hours of practice and honing their skills that these athletes have invested in themselves.

A national newspaper told the story of one super successful golf champion who invested on average 12 hours per day working on his skills. There was another story of a young golfer who spent 11 hours per day at the practice range ONLY working on her short game. It wasn't until she fine-tuned her short game that she stopped and moved onto a different skill.

Writing out goals, practicing affirmations, and embracing the entire process of analyzing, thinking, writing, and rewriting, are all key parts of your Next Level journey. It's similar to the athlete working on their game. Except, unlike that athlete investing 12 hours per day fine-tuning his skills, on this journey, you only need to find 22 minutes in each day.

Your life is your game and only you can decide how you want to play it. On the sidelines, wishing for change or actively engaging in creating the change you desire.

All you have to do is take one small step each day. You CAN create the life of your dreams. I don't want you to dream your life. I want you to live your dream!

To your success – one day at a time!

SECTION ONE
UNDERSTAND YOUR MARVELOUS MIND

Day 1 ◆ Decide to Do Something

Day 2 ◆ Study Gratitude

Day 3 ◆ Learn How to Learn

Day 4 ◆ Discover "Reality"

Day 5 ◆ See How the Mind Matters

Day 6 ◆ Identify Your Support Beams

Day 7 ◆ Choose Who You Will Be

Day 8 ◆ Change Without Blame

Day 9 ◆ Embrace Truth

Day 10 ◆ Make Change Possible

Review

DAY 1
DECIDE TO DO SOMETHING

Begin Each

Day with

Gratitude

Gratitude is a powerful way to begin each day. As you are developing your own "attitude of gratitude," this will not only impact your day, it will impact your whole disposition in life. It will allow you to start the day with a positive outlook, and from a positive outlook comes positive results. I encourage you while you are going through the Next Level Living process to begin each day with gratitude using a gratitude list. It won't take long, and it will help you capture the 10 things you are grateful for.

If you want more – more happiness, better health, more wealth, more love, anything – then commit just a few minutes each day to creating it. Devote this time to your gratitude list and getting clear about the direction in which you want to move for the day.

When you are filling in your day's gratitude list, quickly list 10 things you're grateful for at that moment. Don't over think it, just jot down whatever comes to mind. It can be as simple as the rich cup of coffee in your hand, a family member, or a new job.

Thinking positive thoughts will create positive results. You'll see this for yourself over the course of your journey.

If you start thinking negative thoughts during the day, go back to your gratitude list, ponder it for a moment, take a deep breath and move forward with a hopeful, believing heart. You are making progress, life is wonderful, and everything happens for a reason.

Beginning each day with gratitude is the powerful beginning of your new journey. Now let's get started on your first gratitude list.

For example…

Today, I am grateful for…

1. My decision to make some changes in my life.

2. My supportive husband and wonderful children.

3. A fabulous cup of coffee.

Now write your first gratitude list in your Next Level Living Companion Workbook or notebook.

◆ *Next Level Lesson* ◆
Decide to Do Something

It's not uncommon for some people to be a little skeptical of the idea that you can change just because you decide to, but doesn't everything start with some sort of decision? Even those events that are beyond your control require a decision as to how you will handle them. If you have become aware of something you want to change, your first step is deciding to start. This could be something small and simple to start with, or it may be something life altering. No matter the magnitude, it all starts with a decision. In order to make a difference, you have to make a decision.

There were times in my life when I experienced an "ah-ha moment" and became aware of something that I desperately wanted and/or needed to change. But I let the moment pass, and before I knew it, life crowded in again. At that point it didn't seem so important. We must realize however, that even by choosing not to decide we are making a decision. Sure enough, eventually the issue returns to my awareness, and once again I have to choose. Maybe you have experienced this as well - encountering the cycle of thinking about change, wanting change, but never deciding to do anything about it. Now is your chance to actually make the change you want to see happen! This is the power of Next Level Living.

Take some time to consider your frame of mind. Do you consider yourself to be an optimistic or pessimistic person by nature? Do you trust your decision making skills? Absolutely everything starts with your thoughts. There is tremendous power behind them; power that I will help you tap into during each lesson in this book. Next Level Living will not only educate you on how to tap into the power of your thinking, but will also call you to take action in applying this information - all moving you along in your own personal journey to the next level.

Action

Based on what you have read so far, what does "Next Level Living" mean to you?

Daily Reflection

One person might consider it trivial to make the mad dash to their daughter's school to deliver her dance shoes, however in the eyes of the daughter it was a big deal. A mother can feel a sense of purpose and accomplishment that she was available and had the flexibility to help out her daughter. You must determine for yourself what is trivial and what is not. Don't let someone else judge whether your accomplishments for the day are astronomical or trivial. They are yours, you own them.

Before going to bed, review your gratitude list and reflect on the day's accomplishments. Many times we overlook what we have accomplished because we think it is trivial; but trivial to whom? Look for the good in what you did today. Embrace it and move forward. Tomorrow is a new day, filled with new opportunities.

Now picture the amazing day you will have tomorrow. The most powerful times to feed your subconscious are first thing in the morning and right before you go to sleep. Because when you drift off to sleep with peaceful, positive thoughts, you sleep better and your last thoughts sink deep into your subconscious. This subtly shifts your next day's actions in a way that helps create what you really want out of life.

Jewels for the Journey
Do What it Takes

Repeat these words to yourself often: "I have what it takes." Type them up and hang them on your refrigerator, wall or computer. Look at them each day and believe in yourself. Embrace the changes in your life with a great and expectant attitude. Convince yourself that you can and will do whatever it takes to meet your goals and live the life you dream of. Now be patient! Change doesn't happen overnight. This will take time, but that should not be an excuse to languish along the path to your dreams.

Take time to appreciate who you are right now, and who you want to become. Someday you will look back and be very proud of the decisions that you are making today and the changes you are implementing. Don't fear change or uncertainty. We are usually the most apprehensive about things when we don't have definite outcomes or solutions. But don't give in to worry. Believe that you have the ability to solve any problem that will arise and don't imagine monsters in the closet. You mustn't let the risk of failure keep you from the glorious rewards that await!

DAY 2
STUDY GRATITUDE

Begin Each

Day with

Gratitude

In your companion Next Level Living Workbook, record…

10 things I am grateful for today…

Today, as we embark on day 2 of your Next Level journey, we continue to focus on gratitude, as well as the connection between your thoughts and actions, and the results you see in your life. As you study today's lesson, ask yourself these questions: Do you think life is mostly a random series of events that you have little control over? Or do you believe with the right knowledge and tools, you can learn how to have an impact on the things that "happen to you"?

◆ *Next Level Lesson* ◆
Studies on Gratitude

There is a significant amount of research done on the effects of gratitude. Dr. Robert Emmons (University of California Psychologist and Professor) found that our happiness and positivity are permanently altered by practicing intentional gratitude.

His studies concluded that "participants in a mindset of gratitude felt more joyful, enthusiastic, interested, attentive, energetic, excited, determined and strong." The same participants were also more willing to offer others emotional support.

Participants experiencing gratitude reported sleeping better, increased positive feelings, and increased life satisfaction. They were 25% happier overall than before they began this experiment.

Psychologist Glen Affleck also conducted a study that indicates heart patients "who feel appreciative of life" after a heart attack reduced risks for subsequent attacks.

These studies and others prove that having an "attitude of gratitude" can have very positive physical effects on one's life. How we feel about our lives matters. Being grateful, even for the smallest things, lowers our stress, prevents disease, can extend our lives, and causes us to experience more enjoyment. Expressing gratitude makes those around us feel good as well.

One of the best ways to circumvent negative reactions and thoughts is to focus on those things you are grateful for. Gratitude is one of the most positive emotions we can experience.

If you spend a few moments each day, particularly in the morning, focusing on those things that you are grateful for, it blocks many of the negative emotions you may habitually battle. This is especially helpful at first when you are becoming aware of how much negativity there is in your life.

Gratitude keeps you hopeful and allows you to move forward instead of staying mired in negative thoughts and emotions.

Gratitude creates positive thoughts and thinking positive thoughts creates positive actions, which leads to positive results.

Positive Thoughts → Positive Actions → Positive Results

Action

Expressing gratitude has powerful results. Just as we talked about yesterday, beginning each day with gratitude can have a profound impact on your life. Use this exercise daily for the rest of this book and record what happens in your workbook. You may be surprised! Also, transfer today's gratitude list to something you can carry with you throughout the day reflecting on it often. See how dwelling on the things you are grateful for makes a difference.

Daily Reflection

Before going to bed tonight, review your gratitude list and reflect on the day's accomplishments. Take a moment to feel proud of the time you invested thus far in your journey to the next level. Look for the good in what you did today. Also look closely for any connections between your thoughts, actions, and results. They may not seem evident yet, but know and believe they are there, waiting to reveal themselves further along in your journey.

For now, embrace your accomplishments and move forward. Tomorrow is a new day, filled with new opportunities. As you close your eyes, I want you to visualize the amazing day you will have tomorrow.

DAY 3
LEARN HOW TO LEARN

Begin Each Day with Gratitude

In your companion Next Level Living Workbook record...

10 things I am grateful for today...

Is one of those things you're grateful for today your mind? Barring any special circumstances or an interesting dream you might have had last night, it probably didn't make your top 10 list. Your mind is at work whether you realize it or not. My goal, for the next few days of your journey, is to provide you with a visual representation of how your mind works, so you can make it work ever better for you.

◆ *Next Level Lesson* ◆
How We Learn

From our most formative years, we absorb things around us like a sponge. This is how we gain knowledge and beliefs, and how we start to understand our world. One of the easiest ways to understand the mind is through a simple drawing. (See figure below) This stick figure concept was introduced to me by one of my mentors, Bob Proctor. Bob found it in the work of Dr. Thurman Fleet (the founder of the Concept Therapy Movement). In the 1930s he was a chiropractor and felt that in order to heal his patients in both body and mind, he needed to give them a clear image of the mind. Dr. Fleet believed people think in pictures. And his patients couldn't heal if they didn't have a clear picture of themselves healthy and happy.

With most people, all conscious attention is on their physical body and the physical world. When in fact, everything we experience in our body is actually an expression of our subconscious mind. This is why the body in this diagram is smaller than the mind.

Dr. Fleet's stick person further simplifies this concept by splitting the mind into two main parts – the conscious mind and the subconscious mind. Our conscious mind is the part of the mind that gathers information. It is our thinking mind and is where we can accept, reject, or neglect any idea which presents itself. We use only a small percentage of our conscious mind.

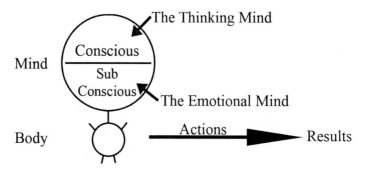

Our subconscious mind is our emotional mind and regulates all bodily sensations, such as taste, touch, sight, hearing and smell. These senses are hardwired in our brain, and they are things which we do not need to think about. Our subconscious mind is also where our habits and belief systems are formed.

The subconscious mind has no ability to reject an idea; it simply accepts every suggestion made to it. The subconscious is also where our memories (good or bad) are stored. This is why when given an exercise to "Think about a dog," an image of a dog immediately comes up for you, and it could be your own lovable pet or the image of your neighbor's vicious guard dog. Regardless, your subconscious pulls up the most ingrained image, and from that image and your personal experiences, emotions are triggered. This in turn provokes your feelings. From the emotional trigger, using the same example, you will either feel warm and fuzzy or frightened when you hear the word "dog" depending on what image your mind brings up. There is a definitive sequence to what occurs. Thoughts create images on the screen of your mind. Those images trigger your emotions and feelings, and those feelings launch your behavior and actions. Your behavior and actions are in direct correlation to the results you are getting in your life.

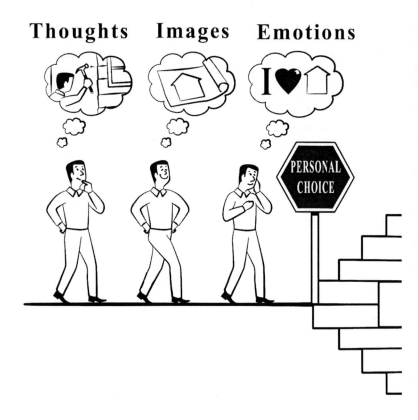

The subconscious mind is the sum total of all our past experiences – what we feel, think and do. It is always working; it's the motor of the mind. The subconscious is what allows us to know and do things instinctively.

Think about the act of walking or riding a bicycle. We all learned to do these things as children and don't have to consciously think about how to do them. Your subconscious mind contains the instructions and can retrieve those instructions, even if it's been ten years since you got on a bicycle. You might wobble at first but after a bit you will successfully peddle and find your balance again.

The reason our mind stores things in this way is to free up the conscious mind to deal with the constant bombardment of stimuli it experiences every day.

If we had to answer email, decide what we wanted for lunch and think about walking and breathing all at the same time, we wouldn't be able to function. So the mind forms patterns of behavior that kick in automatically during certain situations. This is why we seem to get the same results in our lives over and over without really thinking about them or even knowing why.

Action

The positive and negative results in our lives stem from our thought processes.

The realization is that we are getting certain results in our lives – some positive and some negative. Observe how your life looks at this moment. What results are you seeing that you really LIKE? What results are you seeing that you really DON'T LIKE? Jot down a few that come to mind and then return to this list and add to it as you observe your life this week.

Daily Reflection

I hope you enjoyed this peek into the inner workings of your mind. Being aware of the connection between your thoughts, images and emotions is critical to understanding your mind and making the changes you desire.

Now, as you prepare to turn off your mind for some well deserved sleep, it's time to review your gratitude list and reflect on the day's accomplishments. Find the good in what you did today. Embrace it and move forward. Tomorrow is a new day, filled with new opportunities. As you close your eyes tonight, picture the amazing day you will have tomorrow.

DAY 4
DISCOVER "REALITY"

Begin Each

Day with

Gratitude

In your companion Next Level Living Workbook record…

10 things I am grateful for today…

What is your definition of reality? As you continue to understand your marvelous mind today, I want you to consider this question with the understanding that there are no wrong answers.

◆ *Next Level Lesson* ◆
Reality

Thoughts create images on the screen of your mind. Those images trigger your emotions and feelings, and those feelings launch your behavior or actions. Your behavior or actions lead you to results which then produce more thoughts and more feelings. A never-ending cycle exists. You choose however, whether that cycle continues as is or you make changes to it.

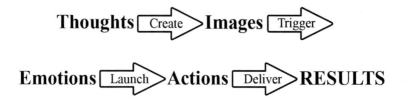

Your brain is really good at keeping you from going insane (although this function can be easily interrupted by your children or spouse). It reminds you of what "reality" is and uses your understanding of "reality" to regulate your actions. For example, you realize that "reality" dictates you cannot fly, and that a high speed impact with the ground would be highly unpleasant. Your brain uses this knowledge to keep you from attempting to fly from the top of the nearest tall building. Because you know it can't be done, this knowledge regulates your behavior.

Most of the time, understanding reality is a good thing. It keeps us safe. This is why you teach your kids to look both ways before crossing the street. You know that a car could injure or kill them, and they may not be aware of this. So you give them a belief to keep them safe, and they believed you even before they truly understood why this is important.

But what if the "reality" that regulates your actions is not "reality" after all? What if it is only your perception of "reality"? Might it still regulate your behavior?

You bet it does! In this case, your brain becomes your worst enemy, because it convinces you of a "reality" that is untrue and limits your possibilities. It was once "reality" that man would never walk on the moon, that Mt. Everest was an insurmountable obstacle and at one time, that the world was flat.

Today, some might consider it "reality" that cancer will never be cured or individuals suffering from paralysis may never walk, simply because our minds convince us that these next levels of reality are beyond our reach.

Take a moment to consider the realities in your life dictated by your mind. Which perceptions are keeping you anchored on your current level? How can you change your mind to turn these limiting beliefs into your own personal walk on the moon?

Action

Looking at the list of results that you wrote down yesterday, consider those you "LIKED" and those you "DIDN'T LIKE." What kind of thinking might be the cause of these results?

Daily Reflection

Before going to bed, review your gratitude list and reflect on the day's accomplishments. Look for the good in what you did today. Embrace your accomplishments and the knowledge you gained today, and visualize it moving you forward to the next level. Tomorrow is a new day, filled with new opportunities. As you close your eyes, picture the amazing day you will have tomorrow.

JEWELS FOR THE JOURNEY
THE POWER OF THE MIND

Brain researcher Susan Greenfield quotes a study done by Harvard in which three groups of non-piano playing adults were placed in three different rooms for a week and given three different tasks regarding playing the piano. The first group was told nothing about the piano in the room, and they were asked just to sit in the room for a week. The second group was given specific instruction on finger exercises for the piano and asked to practice all week. The final group was given the exercises but told only to mentally practice, not actually play the piano.

Subsequently, each of the volunteers underwent a brain scan to determine if there had been any change in brain physiology as a result of the experiment. The first group showed no change from their baseline scans. The second group showed an increase in neuronal activity in the part of the brain that regulates fine motor skills, as a result of practicing the finger exercises. In a stunning result, those who were instructed to simply mentally rehearse the finger exercises showed the highest level of neuronal activity in the brain, even though they had never touched the piano!

This is a big deal! If we spend our time mentally rehearsing the idea that we have nothing to offer, that we are not going to reach our goals, that we are going to fail or anything else negative, our brains record that rehearsal as experience, and the thoughts that flow out of that kind of experience will produce paralyzing feelings of inadequacy and rejection. No wonder so many people fail to live up to their potential. The things they accept as reality might be nothing more than continued habituated limitations in their thinking.

You might realize the need to change your life but be unable to get the process underway, because you believe it is impossible to make any substantive change. If you "know" you can't do it, you won't even make the attempt most of the time. Now is the time to open your heart and mind to a new reality.

DAY 5
SEE HOW THE MIND MATTERS

Begin Each

Day with

Gratitude

In your companion Next Level Living Workbook record...

10 things I am grateful for today...

Are you having trouble coming up with 10 new things to feel gratitude for every day? There are no rules against repetition. In fact, repetition is a key part of your journey to the Next Level of Living. This is especially true of those days along the way when, despite your best efforts and intentions, it seems like you're stuck in molasses, not making any perceptible progress.

Stick with it (no pun intended)! Keep journaling, even if you find you're repeating yourself, continue reading each lesson and uncovering the jewels buried within that relate to your journey, and embrace each action exercise as an opportunity for a breakthrough that will "unstick" you and propel your forward.

Embrace repetition, even when it comes to writing your daily gratitude lists. Gratitude is a powerful emotion that will not be dampened by lack of originality. As you begin each day of your journey with gratitude, write from your heart not your head.

◆ *Next Level Lesson* ◆
The Mind Matters

Most people look at their results as their potential. This is not accurate. The results we have been getting up until now are merely a reflection of our past thoughts and actions. Once we learn to paint beautiful pictures in our mind of what we want, our results will reflect this change.

This process must start with the conscious mind where, as we mentioned earlier, you gather information and make choices. Remember this is the part of the mind that has the ability to accept, reject or ignore ideas. We have to understand that we have been influenced by our environment through our five senses our entire lives. Information is fed into our conscious mind through our senses. When we were very young (up to about age six) our conscious mind wasn't completely developed. We absorbed what we experienced as reality, because we didn't have any sort of filter to interpret the world at that point. The ideas and beliefs of others were fed directly into our subconscious mind. This created the "buttons" that now cause us to react (and others often now know how to push).

These beliefs now sit in our subconscious mind affecting the image of ourselves and altering our perception of the world around us, including our thoughts about what is possible. This part of our mind has no choice but to accept what we think. Fixed ideas will then continue to express themselves without conscious assistance until they are replaced. These are your thought habits. However, you can create new positive habits simply through repetition. As I discussed in today's opener, no matter how much you feel like banging your head against the wall in frustration, keep at it. Steadfastly follow the roadmap set forth for each of these days of your journey. This type of repetition is reprogramming your mind to think differently and when you think differently, the results you produce will also be different than the ones you're used to.

The Power to Choose

We each have the power to choose the direction of our lives. Not only do you deserve the best life possible, so does your family. As parents, we pass down our physical attributes and assets to our children, but we also pass down our mindsets and beliefs. Some are helpful and encouraging, and others that are destructive. In order to understand how to change some of these destructive patterns, we have to understand how these beliefs affect us and then understand how our mind forms new beliefs.

Many people think they don't have much, if any, choice in how things turn out in their life. They live with a fatalistic sense of the world, as in "My family has never gone to college, so it's not meant for me to either." Or, "I've never lived anywhere else, so I can't move, no matter how bad things are here." By not identifying their basic belief systems and not taking responsibility for their actions, these people continue to make poor choices that affect themselves, their children, their grandchildren, and entire generations to follow.

The good news is that the opposite is true as well. You have the power to instill confidence and love in those around you, by simply choosing to do so.

I've found this to be the case with my own children. Though I had some ingrained thought patterns from my childhood, I actively chose not to pass those on to my children. What you pass on to others is entirely your choice.

Our Minds Can Adapt To Anything

It may surprise you to know that the ability to adapt and exist in difficult circumstances is a basic human survival skill. The human mind is a fabulous tool. It has amazing coping skills to allow us to exist and survive under adverse circumstances.

Animals have this skill as well. A good example of this is what happens to circus elephants.

A man once went to the circus with his young daughter. He was surprised when he saw a group of eight elephants and found that each was tethered by only a small rope attached to a ring on an iron leg shackle. Each of the small ropes was tied to a much larger rope that was staked to the ground. The ropes and stakes were no match for the size and strength of the elephant. Any one of them could have easily walked away to explore the nearby shopping mall. The man couldn't help but wonder why they didn't break free, so he questioned the trainer.

He discovered that when they are very young, elephants are chained by the leg to immovable stakes. For several weeks, they struggle to free themselves. Little by little, they come to the realization that they can't move about freely when they are tied by the right rear leg. The elephants at the circus didn't roam around because they believed they couldn't. Being six tons, they could have easily broken free, however the tethers in their minds were stronger than any chain or rope.

The same type of coping mechanism is at work with prisoners of war. If held in captivity long enough, they begin to perceive their world in the context of prison life, and thoughts of escape or going back to a regular life fade away. They cope with daily life, torture, and constant abuse by becoming immune to the horror of it. Eventually it becomes their new reality and they don't consciously think of it anymore. They settle into acceptance.

This is also true to a much lesser degree in our own daily life. If you hear others frequently tell you what you can't do, you become convinced and adapt to those limits. Though external sources may affect your ideas of who you are, the worst and most resistant source of criticism comes from within – from the ingrained belief systems you acquired and developed in your own mind.

Action

Today I want you to write at least three old beliefs you have and then craft the new beliefs you would like to replace them with. Here are some additional examples to get you thinking:

Old Beliefs	New Beliefs
Terrible with Money	I am successfully working on my money management skills
Can't lose weight	I am maintaining a healthy weight
Can't cook	I am easily creating a delicious meal
Can't run a business	I am learning and applying helpful business skills

Now it is your turn. Create a list of your old beliefs and the new beliefs to replace them.

Daily Reflection

Before going to bed, review the gratitude list that came from your heart this morning and reflect on your accomplishments and next level lessons learned today. Look for the good in your day, embrace it and move forward. Tomorrow is a new day, filled with new opportunities. As you close your eyes, picture the amazing day you will have tomorrow.

DAY 6
IDENTIFY YOUR SUPPORT BEAMS

Begin Each Day with Gratitude

In your companion Next Level Living Workbook record...

10 individuals I am grateful for today...

Did you notice the change in wording above? Today, we will be identifying the support beams in your life, many of them being the people who surround and support you. I thought it only fitting to start by acknowledging gratitude for some of those individuals.

◆ *Next Level Lesson* ◆
Support Beams

We all have different people, places, things or activities we can turn to when we experience challenging or transitional times in our lives. I like to call these our support beams. These support beams can come in a variety of forms. Family, friends, and coworkers are the most common, but they can also be pets, places, activities or things that lift your spirits. (See Appendix A for a list of some of my favorites.) Any and all of these people, things and activities can help support you as you change your life. I encourage you to think about your own personal support beams and learn to lean on them without fear when you need the extra boost. This can be anything that comforts or frees your mind – things like cooking, reading, fishing, golf, or just a good old Sunday afternoon nap! Or maybe it is connecting with your close friends or family.

Once you identify your own support beams, you will recognize there will be times where you will utilize different support beams for different situations. There is the story of a young lady who experienced some challenges in an unhealthy relationship with a boyfriend. This young lady knew she was the one who personally needed to confront the challenges yet needed support from her trusted advisors to end the relationship. In this particular situation, the support beams she turned to were people who supported her. Another person in the same situation might turn to different support beams, perhaps taking a quiet vacation with time for much needed rest and to clear one's thoughts before moving forward. A business executive I know utilizes exercise as a support beam to help clear his thoughts, rather than his counterpart who enjoys curling up in front of a fire wrapped up in a warm blanket. Regardless of which support beams you turn to, trust that the ones you choose are the right ones for that moment.

You are nearly one week into the process of change at the core of your next level journey. You have seen that change is not something that happens overnight. Now is the time to fully equip yourself with the support you need for your journey to the next level.

No man is an island

On your journey to change your mindset, it is very helpful to find a friend or group of people who want to change too, so you can offer support to one another. It is very important to be mindful of the people who you spend time with during this critical part of your journey. You need encouragement and support, not ridicule or discouragement. If that means you have to spend less time around certain family members or friends, then you must make that choice. Once you are more confident and strong, their negativity won't bother you as much. You have the choice whether to absorb someone else's negative ideas or set them aside. If you find yourself in a situation you can't easily remove yourself from, you can consciously choose to reject their words.

The English poet and philosopher, John Donne, wrote, "No man is an island." This means that each of our interactions with another person connects and ripples across multiple lives. Every conversation and every action affects one person and that person's impression of us. In turn, they interact with other people in a way that reflects that impression. Realizing the tremendous impact you have on other people, and the impact they have on you and everything you do, puts the importance of maintaining healthy relationships into perspective. Working diligently and purposefully to establish positive relationships can be key in creating the thoughts, actions, and results you desire in life.

Action

Make a list of your support beams. What and who will keep you uplifted and motivated as you strive to make changes in your life?

Daily Reflection

Before going to bed, review your list of people you are grateful for, your complete support beams list from today's action, and then reflect on the day's accomplishments. Look for the good in what you did today – what happened today that made you smile just thinking about it now? Embrace that feeling and move forward. Tomorrow is a new day, filled with new opportunities. As you close your eyes, picture the amazing day you will have tomorrow.

DAY 7
CHOOSE WHO YOU WILL BE

Begin Each

Day with

Gratitude

In your companion Next Level Living Workbook record...

10 things I am grateful for today...

Consider this...

> *Growing in Life is knowing when to PUSH &*
> *when to just be PATIENT.*
> — *Linda McLean*

◆ *Next Level Lesson* ◆
You Choose Who You Will Be

How we talk to ourselves sends a powerful message to our "internal self," which directly impacts the results we get. Throughout the day, observe how you talk to yourself about yourself. When you catch yourself thinking something negative or less than desirable about yourself, STOP right there! Choose to speak positive words that help change the images on the screen of your mind to a new channel: the new, positive YOU channel. Practice some kindness toward yourself and stop beating yourself up for the past. Focus on today and what you can accomplish. Give yourself a little pep talk that you can do it!

On the other end of the spectrum from can, is the word can't – a four letter word. From now on, you have to treat it as such. We are conditioned from early childhood to live within a set of limitations and expectations created for us, largely by others. Most of these people had our best interests at heart. Even though they may have loved us deeply and cared for our well-being, some of the beliefs they passed down were not very helpful. If those beliefs about our own abilities are outdated or no longer serve our interests, they need to be tossed out like yesterday's horrible pasta salad.

Today you choose your own "reality." You can have the one you were given or you can choose another. If the views you were given fit your mother, grandmother, sister, teachers, father, or best friend, but they don't fit you, give them back! You have the absolute right to decide how you will view yourself and the world around you.

Action

With an open, forgiving mind, I want you to write in your workbook or on a piece of paper, a list of everyone you can think of who gave you those old beliefs about yourself – the ones that have only limited you (we talked about them on Day 5). These things are often the cause of great hurt or lack of action in our lives. Without being angry about it or wanting vengeance, just write it down. For example, you might write, "My father told me I would never be good at writing poetry, and I should find something else to do." This might be painful to write, but with great courage and a non-judgmental attitude, just write it down.

Maybe someone in your life told you that you are terrible with money, can't cook, can't run a business, can't lose weight, or aren't a public speaker; whatever the belief, if it doesn't serve you, think about where it came from and include it on your list. Some of us have long lists, and some short ones. The length is not important because just one untrue belief can have drastic effects on how we think and feel about ourselves.

When you have finished, simply look at the list and in your own heart (or out loud), give those limitations back to the person who handed them to you. For example, "Dad, I am giving you back this limiting belief, because it does not serve me. I think I can write beautiful poetry if I practice and learn." Do the same for each belief and each person. Most of the time, these people actually meant well and did not intend to harm you. Some did, of course, but we are not trying to decipher motives here or assign blame, only giving them back that which does not fit the person you want to become.

Now, who gave you old beliefs? What did they say or do (or not do) that sent you a limiting message? Now in your own heart (or out loud), give those limitations back to the person who gave them to you.

Daily Reflection

Before going to bed, review your gratitude list and congratulate yourself on your accomplishments today. Look for the good in what you did today. Embrace the freedom and sense of lightness you feel from giving back your old beliefs and move forward with the new ones you've replaced them with. Tomorrow is a new day, filled with new opportunities. As you close your eyes, picture the amazing day you will have tomorrow.

DAY 8
CHANGE WITHOUT BLAME

Begin Each

Day with

Gratitude

In your companion Next Level Living Workbook record...

10 things I am grateful for today

(and today be sure to include the areas of your life that you consider works in progress)...

If you were a house, what kind would you be? Brand new, modern, classic, or a fixer-upper? Many people overlook the beauty and possibilities of a fixer upper, failing to see it as an opportunity for creativity and problem solving. If you were a fixer-upper, which things about yourself would you classify as works in progress, each with the potential for greatness?

◆ *Next Level Lesson* ◆
Change without Blame

I am the primary designer and crafter of my own life. I can redecorate, remodel, or rebuild it to suit me, no matter my age or experience. Most of us have lived in places that needed one or all of these kinds of efforts to make them livable. Sometimes all that is needed is redecorating, a kind of sprucing up, making changes that are mostly cosmetic to reflect changes in style or direction. A homemaker, a businessperson, or university student might be completely satisfied with the overall direction of their life but see the need to make some alterations to better address a changing situation.

The new homemaker, who realizes she might suddenly end up with too much time on her hands, could decide that while a career isn't the answer, that time could be well used volunteering at the local hospital. The businessperson might decide that they need to upgrade their computer skills to keep up with technology changes in the workplace. A university student might choose to change the group of friends they are hanging around with, to increase their productivity by decreasing peer pressure to waste time on things that don't move them forward. These kinds of changes do not require any major structural alteration, just an "upgrade."

But sometimes we need to remodel. There are circumstances that dictate more significant changes in the configuration of our lives, without really having to take it down to the ground. This is when a moderate shift or change will produce the desired result. A promotion at work, for example, which would require a shift in responsibilities and the way in which you work, would be an example of a remodel.

Finally, unfortunately, under some conditions, we need to completely rebuild. The loss of a life partner to death or divorce might require that we rebuild a whole new life, one that fits our new reality. A major health issue could leave us with few options and require that we reconfigure the bulk of our life. The reasons are many, but when we are faced with life altering situations, they often require life altering solutions.

In my own case, a major health issue required me to rebuild my life in a way that I did not anticipate and initially protested. When it came time to undergo radiation treatments, the doctor told me that I MUST stop and rest in order for the treatments to be effective. In my business, I had developed a bad habit of not having many boundaries in my work day. I tried to explain to the doctor that my clients needed me, and I had to be available. How could I possibly find time to rest in the middle of the day? My sister sitting beside me listening to the doctor's orders took one LONG look at me and said "You have to make some changes and it has to be NOW!"

My doctor also made it clear that this was not a negotiation. In order to give my body the time to heal, the best prescription was rest. This was a huge wake up call for me; one that I'd never had to face before. Nobody (including myself) had ever dared try to slow me down. But this time, altering my life in the face of this life-altering situation was required.

I followed doctor's orders and rearranged my schedule – and stopped. What resulted was much more than a change of schedule; it was a change of mindset that I've kept with me ever since. I let go of the reality I previously knew and made my own health and healing the center of my own world. Along with my family in that center, this continues to be how I prioritize my life today.

Stop the Blame Game

It has, unfortunately, become socially acceptable to blame others for our circumstances. It's especially tempting to believe and act as though there is some other person to whom we can look, either as the cause of our specific situation or as the person somehow responsible for fixing it.

We are the ones who choose the lives we have, and we are the ones who have the power to change those lives. Our past will influence the person we are, but we are not required to be the victim of our circumstances. Even if our circumstances are of our own design. To think otherwise is to limit ourselves to that which is and to ignore that which can be. Such a victim mentality ultimately leaves us powerless and vulnerable. It leaves us unable to choose or to affect outcomes.

We need to remember the forces that made us the person we are, but from the standpoint of where we currently are. Only then can we learn, grow, and redirect our energies into a different channel that better aligns with the level we wish to ascend.

Obviously, no one consciously chooses to be in an abusive relationship, a dead end job, or in some kind of behavioral bear trap such as addiction. If that's where you find yourself, you can now consciously choose to either remain trapped there in the dark or turn on the flashlight and move out of it. Of course, there will be consequences to your choices, but there are always consequences. There are consequences for refusing to read the handwriting on the wall and adapt or change to what you know to be true. Try as we might to escape it, the fact remains, we are living the life we have, because we choose to. We can choose a different staircase aimed toward different outcomes, but that's entirely up to us. There is no one else responsible for our lives.

If it is to be, it is up to me!

Action

Now you might need to learn how to choose differently. Old habits of thought and behavior are going to die hard in some situations. You might need to learn some new skills, find new friends or simply focus on what you really want. But it must begin with the understanding that you can change your way of thinking and thereby change your feelings and actions. It cannot begin in any other way, since the way you feel and the way you behave flows from how you think.

In looking at all the areas of your own life (personal, work, spiritual, etc.) what do you WANT to redecorate, remodel or rebuild in your life and why? Keep in mind what you want isn't the same as what you need. Needs are food, water, and other basics for survival.

For example: After assessing the various areas of your life, you may come to the conclusion that one of your work goals needs a redecoration (perhaps improving your time management skills), one of your relationships needs remodeling (the person you're dating is becoming an emotional strain for instance), and your spiritual life needs a rebuild (starting a habit of daily prayer and meditation needs to occur for the very first time).

Daily Reflection

Before going to bed, review your list of personal works in progress you are grateful for and reflect on the day's accomplishments. Reflect on the good in what you did today and visualize moving toward your Next Level of Living. Embrace the feeling of forward momentum as you decide to redecorate, remodel or rebuild various areas of your life. Tomorrow is a new day filled with new opportunities. As you close your eyes, picture the amazing day you will have tomorrow.

DAY 9
EMBRACE TRUTH

Begin Each

Day with

Gratitude

In your companion Next Level Living Workbook record…

10 things I am grateful for today…

Here is one quote I am personally grateful for whenever I hear it:

> *If you can dream it, you can do it.*
> -Walt Disney

◆ *Next Level Lesson* ◆
Embrace Truth

There is a tendency to resist writing things out that we do not believe to be true. It feels dishonest and maybe self-deceptive (or just plain awkward). In reality, it is no different than what we told ourselves as a baby learning to walk. The baby sees others walking and believes that she can do it too. Armed with the belief, "I can walk" she sets about the task of falling down repeatedly but never abandons the belief. When she begins crashing into the furniture, she presses on because in her heart she knows her belief is true. Eventually her life will reflect that truth, even though it did not at first. We are doing much the same here. You have likewise been conditioned to think in certain ways, and we need to change that thinking. It might sound untrue right up to the point that it becomes your new "reality."

After you experience this a few times, and see things in your life come to pass that are positive and move you forward toward your Next Level of Living, you will start to embrace your new ideas as truth immediately, even before you see them happen. If everyone stood around and only believed that which they could see, we would never achieve great things. We must be able to imagine a better life and then strive for it to become our truth.

Think about the person you are becoming. You are limitless and brave. You are powerful and able to choose for yourself. You are capable and venturesome. You are amazing. That's you! You just need to run into the coffee table a few times before you are fully convinced.

Wanting Too Much

I frequently see people stop themselves from dreaming too big, wanting too much, or living better than they think they should. Why? Who's to say what dream is too big or how much money is too much or which job is out of your reach? Why do we actively choose to limit ourselves?

A good example of this is Jennifer, a graduating senior from Duke University, President of the Christian Intervarsity League and a Mexican American. Her father's belief system had a powerful effect on her life. She shares her story:

"My mother has always been big on education so I always assumed I would go to college. My parents divorced when I was little, and when I got into high school I asked my dad what he thought about college. He told me that college

was a waste for girls, and I needed to settle down and find a good man. I was devastated. Though I now realize that he spoke out of fear, since he'd never been to college, and he didn't want to see me fail, it still hurt.

I determined that I would go anyway but the idea that I was expecting too much and might ultimately fail was lodged in my mind. This became my picture of myself – a little hopeful but still fatalistic on some level. When I got accepted into Duke, I told my mom that I had decided to go to Texas Tech instead. It was only a couple of hours from home and most of my friends were going there. She was shocked and upset that I chose to limit my options when one of the greatest opportunities of my life lay within my grasp. After much arguing, she convinced me to spend at least one semester at Duke, and if I didn't like it, I could come home.

Needless to say, I came to North Carolina and never looked back. I am so grateful that I didn't let my dad's words keep me from experiencing all the great things that I've been through at Duke these past four years. It was okay for me to let dad keep his limited belief. I understand now he owns those beliefs, not me."

People develop their beliefs about what they can or can't accomplish from even the smallest incidents or comments like Jennifer experienced. Words spoken out of fear by a parent when she was just a teen, could have limited her whole outlook on what she could accomplish and who she might become.

This may have happened to you in the past. You may have allowed a parent's (or spouse's) negative comments convince you that you can't do something. You may still have family or friends that constantly tell you to quit dreaming and focus on "reality." You have to decide if you will let them limit your life and keep you in that dark basement. It may not feel like a conscious choice but it is. You can choose at any time to stop giving them power over your life, over your dreams.

Knowing that you are in control of your own destiny, no matter what others say, gives you the freedom to find your true self and determine who you will become from this point forward.

Ultimate Dream List

Now that you have decided you want to make a change in your life and embrace Next Level Living, you have to figure out what it is that you really want. Now is the time for you to visualize what it will be like to walk up that staircase into the light.

You need to give yourself permission to dream like you did when you were a child – as if the sky is the limit and anything is possible. As we get older, we tend to stop dreaming like we used to. We limit our dreams to our current version of what is "do-able" instead of really pushing ourselves toward greatness. In the Action step for today, in the spirit of Mr. Disney, you will have the freedom to dream it, document it and then make the decision to do it!

Once you have written down your dreams and then review what you wrote, it will bring clarity to your decision making. You can then decide if you actually want what you wrote or not.

After all we don't DREAM our life, we should LIVE our dream. The BE, DO, & HAVE lists that follow are critical at the beginning of this journey of taking your life to the next level. It is from these lists that you will determine your true goals and then set specific actions that will lead to achieving those goals.

Action

Spend time dreaming. Create your "Ultimate Personal Dream List." This list has three parts:

Who you want to BE (or become) before you leave this earth; what you want to DO; and what you want to HAVE. Let your imagination roam far and wide as you think of every single area

---

of your life. Now write down 10 items on your own BE, DO and HAVE lists. The ULTIMATE list should have 30 items on each list, but to get started, write down at least 10. The reason to write 30 or more is that it causes you to think outside the box, allowing your mind to expand beyond its normal boundaries. See Appendix B for examples from my Be, Do and Have lists to get your thinking revved up.

Review your lists and start really contemplating the items you've written. We will soon start setting goals that will stem from these lists, but for now just imagine what your life would be like if you received everything on your lists. How amazing and inspiring would it be to live on that level. And the best part is that you have the power to make it happen!

Daily Reflection

Before going to sleep tonight and allowing your subconscious mind to dream as big as it wants to, review your gratitude list and reflect on the day's accomplishments. Look for the good in what you did today. Embrace it all and move forward. Tomorrow is a new day, filled with new opportunities. As you close your eyes, picture the amazing day you will have tomorrow.

DAY 10
MAKE CHANGE POSSIBLE

Begin Each Day with Gratitude

In your companion Next Level Living Workbook record…

10 habits I am grateful for today…

That's right, habits. Think of 10 things you do on a regular basis that you feel contribute positively to your Next Level Living journey.

◆ *Next Level Lesson* ◆
Make Change Possible

You have the power to get different results in your life by changing your thinking. It may sound simple, but it's not. Your thought patterns have existed within you for a long time, and it takes a great deal of persistence and work to change them.

In 1995 I attended one of Bob Proctor's seminars. One exercise he challenged us to undertake was to change one thing we were conditioned to do. It was to prove to us that if we were serious about bringing about change, we could do it! Specifically, Bob challenged us to move our watch (everyone wore them back then) from the wrist we generally wore it on, to the other wrist. In my case it was moving it from my left wrist (which is where my parents wore their watches) to my right wrist. In the seminar, we all moved our watches and the challenge began. Of course, at first it was awkward. Frequently my eyes went looking for the watch on my left wrist, and I had to adjust my gaze to the right. The next difference I noticed was getting into the routine each morning of purposefully putting it on my right wrist. This required focused thinking and coordination instead of habitual action. I was determined to prove to myself that I would not default into my old pattern. Time passed, and somewhere between 45 and 60 days, I realized I had developed a different habit. I have heard others state it takes on average 22 days to develop a new habit, so I must be in the category of a highly spirited and difficult horse to break – but I did make the change!

Today, over 15 years later, I am still wearing my watch on my right wrist. The interesting twist to this whole exercise is that if you look at my daughter Brittany's watch, you will find it on her right wrist as well. So the exercise not only showed me that I do have the ability to make changes, but that I also have the power of influence. When we do something purposeful, it may be that others are influenced without us being purposeful about influencing them!!

Action

Which of your habits (where you wear your watch, the sock you usually put on first, how you start each morning, etc) would you be willing to change? For the next 10 days make the change in this habit and document what you learn from the whole process. This exercise is simply to prove to yourself that you can create change in your life.

Daily Reflection

Before going to bed, review your list of positive habits and reflect on how they contributed to the day's accomplishments. Celebrate the results you saw (no result is too small to be called a victory), embrace the feeling of winning and move forward. Tomorrow is a new day, filled with new opportunities. As you close your eyes, picture the amazing day you will have tomorrow.

JEWELS FOR
THE JOURNEY
FORGED WITH FIRE

You can think of your life as similar to a diamond. Diamonds were created very early in the earth's history through the exertion of great pressure and force. If you think of your life, it is much the same. Over time we go through great pressures and forces that have an effect on our lives. As a result we are shaped and formed into the person we become.

As you think of your life, you know that the best things in life don't just happen to appear magically. If we just coast through our lives, accepting what comes rather than choosing to create our experiences, there are many things that we will miss out on or not experience fully. The process of creating your life takes effort and there will be times you will wonder if it's really worth it, but you must focus on the diamond and not allow a little pressure to scare you off.

Just as a diamond has to go through the process of mining, cutting, cleaning, and polishing, leaving behind "waste" if it is to become the brilliant gem that it is, this process is true for us as well. We must remove the old ideas, attitudes, and clutter before we can move ahead. It can be something as simple as a stack of old bills we haven't thrown out or a closet full of clothes that no longer fit. It can be an unhealthy relationship we have continued in because it's easier than breaking it off, or an unhealthy habit we haven't had the courage to address. In order to create change, we must make room for it in our lives. This means that some of the old clutter, actions, and ideas have to go. Old thoughts, behaviors, and even relationships may have to be removed. To decide what needs to be adjusted in your life, create a list of the things and situations that you are currently tolerating. What will it take to eliminate each one? Change is possible – but only if you clear a path for it.

REVIEW

You are now at your first "check point" to find out how the journey to your Next Level of Living is progressing. Congratulations on all you have accomplished in just a few days!

Here is what you have accomplished so far...

◆ You've started each day focusing on what you are grateful for.

◆ You've determined what Next Level Living means to you.

◆ You've taken some time to document the results in your life that you LIKE and those that you DON'T LIKE.

◆ You've investigated the thinking underlying these results.

◆ You've identified your Old Beliefs and determined your New Beliefs.

◆ You've gathered your list of Support Beams.

◆ You've identified who gave you your Old Beliefs and you've made the effort to mentally give them back.

◆ You've decided IF you are going to Redecorate, Remodel or Rebuild the various areas of your life.

◆ You've dreamed and documented your Be, Do and Have Lists.

◆ You have realized change is possible!

If you have not already done so, now is the perfect time to check on the website (www.nextlevellivingbook.com) for the free resources we offer to help you on your way.

SECTION TWO
CHART YOUR COURSE

Jewels for
the Journey
Awareness, Acceptance,
Action & Accountability

The reason you figure out "what is" in your life, and then assess your personality and the personalities around you is to create an awareness of who you are, where you are and what situations you are dealing with. Only by becoming aware of what is really going on and taking accountability for your role in it, can you begin to take action to change and improve.

It is vital to take responsibility for all areas of your life, as you can't change anything you don't feel responsible for. While it may seem a little scary to take on the burden for every part of your life you want to improve, it is actually very empowering. As you become convinced that you do have choices and can make the changes you desire, you will be naturally propelled forward to get the results you really want at your Next Level of Living.

You are the designer and architect of your own future and no matter what has happened or what you have experienced in the past, there is no limit to what you can and will experience in the future.

You can sit at your kitchen table right now and start your own process of figuring out "what is." Don't wait until your birthday, New Year's Eve, or any other future, arbitrary moment in time to start charting your course – now is the time to start your process of change.

The first step is awareness which is to get clear on how you think about things. This means to be aware of your thoughts and your reactions to events or situations. Often, we just go through our days reacting without consciously thinking about why we react the way we do. We live our lives on autopilot, so the first step is to power down the autopilot and examine where your thoughts are and how that is affecting your life.

Once you become aware of what you are thinking and how this has been affecting your results, you must accept "what is." Where you are right now is neither good nor bad so you have to resist feeling overwhelmed, being highly demanding or justifying your behavior. Acceptance brings relief when you embrace it because it allows you to start moving forward.

The next step is to make a plan. If you were going to drive from San Francisco to New York, would you map out your path? Think of the captain of a sailboat, if he doesn't chart his path across the waters, he would drift aimlessly and likely not make it to his desired destination. The captain is constantly aware of the shifting winds, the turbulent waters, and makes the necessary adjustments along the way. So once you are aware of how you are thinking about what you want in your life, it starts to send a strong message out as to what you want to change. Then once you completely accept where you are at right now, even though you might not be too proud of where you are, you accept it and are ready to clearly articulate what your plan will look like to achieve your future goals.

The last key portion that makes this work is action coupled with accountability. You must think about what it will take to achieve your goals. What must be set aside in order to achieve what you really want? Does something need to be sacrificed? If so, what? You can't make room in your life to accomplish new goals if you don't set aside some current activities or behaviors. Let's remember that it may only require a temporary reprieve from these activities; just enough time to achieve the goal at hand. You hold the power to add or delete actions in your life, and it's up to you to make it happen. You know yourself best and therefore know how you want to invest your time, and who is best qualified to protect your time and set your priorities? You!

The lessons and tools you are receiving throughout your Next Level journey in this book are specifically designed to guide you through this process of change and accountability. In the previous section, you learned how your mind works. Now, let's chart your course to success!

DAY 11
FIND OUT "WHAT IS"

Begin Each

Day with

Gratitude

In your companion Next Level Living Workbook, record…

10 things I am grateful for today…

As you begin to chart the course of your Next Level Living journey, think about all the different people, circumstances and other seemingly random events that have contributed to charting the course of your life so far. Now, imagine a line representing the map of your life so far. I'll bet it has far more twists and turns than stretches of solid, straight, unbending road, doesn't it? Of course it does! Unexpected detours, often leading to wonderful surprises, are some of the most beautiful things about life. Be grateful for each one but be sure that you are the captain of the ship at the helm when making such detours. Don't be a rudderless boat, without any oars drifting in circles.

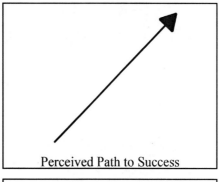

Perceived Path to Success

Realistic Path to Success

◆ *Next Level Lesson* ◆
What Is

In order to build on your BE, DO, and HAVE lists you must continue to gain clarity on what really matters to you – not to me or anyone else and not what you think is supposed to matter, but what really matters to you as an individual.

In order to have any idea where you are going, you must first evaluate where you are now. This should be done as objectively as possible without self-judgment or negativity. This is about taking an honest look at where you are in life, not about where you think you should be based on prior dreams you had for yourself or mistakes made along the way. It is about creating a new life. In order to do this you must build on where you are right now.

Look at life as a wonderful journey. If you were to set out on a journey in your car but had no idea where you were, how would you ever know how to get to your destination? We're all different and start in different places. That doesn't mean where you are starting is any better or worse than anyone else. It is just different. It is like a dot on the map that represents where you are in life or the infamous "You are Here" red circle on a shopping mall map.

If we were all in the same place at the same time, after all, wouldn't it be kind of crowded in that spot? Determine your personal starting point without attaching any emotions or regrets to it. When you think about the current state of your life, what are the first thoughts that come to your mind?

I recently heard about Heather from Texas. She'd been an executive secretary for more than fifteen years, yet she felt as if she was trapped in a big fat rut. Heather is beautiful, funny, well-educated, and cultured. From the outside, it looks like she leads a fabulous life. She said,

> *"I feel like I'm in that movie Groundhog Day where I live every day just like the day before. Nothing is really wrong; it's just that I'm sick of doing it. I go to the same places, talk to the same people, deal with the same issues and then it starts all over again. You know, I thought when I was thirty that this life was perfect. All my friends were married and had toddlers clinging to their skirts, and I was free to do as I pleased, but now that I look back on these last seven years, what have I done? I feel like life is passing me by, but I don't know exactly what to do about it. I just know I don't want to keep feeling this way."*

Heather was starting to take inventory of her life. This is the first step in choosing something different and rewriting your roadmap to Next Level Living. Does it mean you suddenly have a clear understanding of what you want, and it's off to the races, just like that? No. It just means that you have found the race track and made it to the starting line, something many people never do.

Now that you've arrived here, it's time to stop living in the past and penalizing yourself for the results of past races. Let go of the past! Today is the day to start anew!

Action

For this exercise, leave your emotions at the door and as objectively as possible write down "what is" in each of the eight areas of life listed below. Include those things that are good in your life as well as those you want to change. Jot down the first things that come to mind. Remember, no labeling them as good or bad.

"What is"...

...in the Personal Growth area of my life?

...in the Health area of my life?

...in the Relationship area of my life?

...in the Finance area of my life?

...in the Business/Career/or Education area of my life?

...in the Spiritual area of my life?

...in the Recreational area of my life?

...in the Community area of my life?

Daily Reflection

Before going to bed tonight, review your gratitude list and reflect on the day's accomplishments. Look for the good in all areas of your life. Embrace the feeling of taking steps forward in your journey. Tomorrow is a new day, filled with new opportunities and wonderful surprises. As you close your eyes, picture the amazing day you will have tomorrow.

DAY 12
SEE HOW YOU GOT HERE

Begin Each

Day with

Gratitude

In your companion Next Level Living Workbook, record…

10 things I am grateful for today…

*Actions speak louder than words, so believe what
you see and forget what you heard.*
                                        -Source Unknown

◆ *Next Level Lesson* ◆
How Did I Get Here?

I often speak with people who gaze at their "what is" list and wonder, "How did I get here?" We all start our adult lives with ideas of how our life will go and where we might be when we reach 30, 40, 50, or 60 years old. Invariably we get to that age and think, "I thought it would be different. It doesn't look the way I imagined it." Sometimes this is good in that we have achieved more than we ever dreamed, but other times it is negative, and we feel like hamsters on a wheel just trying to keep up with the pace and stress of life.

A friend recently met Janine at a seminar. Her first words were, *"I can't figure out how I ended up living my mother's life! I worked hard, got my degree, married and had kids. Now, fifteen years later, I feel like I'm just the maid, chauffeur, sidekick, and assistant. I used to have a less-than-positive view of my mother, because it seemed all she did was cook and clean and help my dad. Now I'm neck deep in this crazy life and feel like I've stepped into my mother's life!"*

How did this happen? It's important to recognize that the life you live right now has been influenced by the people, experiences and choices from your past. As a child you gained knowledge and experience from the people who raised you. You were also influenced by teachers, schoolmates, and other authority figures such as grandparents, church or club leaders. One of the great books I read while raising my daughters was *Children Are Wet Cement* by Anne Ortlund. This image of wet cement serves as the perfect example of how impressionable children are.

People, places and experiences in our lives have shaped us all at some level into who we are today. No one ends up with a life that is somehow disconnected from these influences. Now is the time to evaluate who is influencing you and make a shift accordingly.

Jim Rohn taught that we become the combined average of the five people we hang around the most. The people we spend our time with determine what conversations dominate our attention, and what observations, attitudes and opinions we repetitively are introduced to. He suggests we think of our influences in three different categories, which are:

1. **Disassociation** – This is the hardest, but sometimes the most necessary. By deciding what you want for your life, you will gain clarity on the influence this person has on you, and if by continuing to associate with them it will serve your ultimate purpose, vision, and dreams. In most cases of disassociation, the

answer is overwhelmingly "no." This is when you must decide what is more important – associating with this person or continuing unencumbered on your journey to the next level.

2. **Limited Associations** – This category is for the people you can spend five minutes with or even five hours with, but not five days, and certainly NOT five weeks! When you think of your time as an investment, this is the category in which you decide how much you can "afford" to be influenced, based on how these people represent themselves.

3. **Expanded Associations** – This category is like your dream team. Based on which area(s) of your life you want to take to the next level, find those people who represent the success you want. Success is simple, it just takes purpose to move to the next level. Good role models can help serve this purpose. Surround yourself with people who have more success in a certain area of life than you currently do. Take a look at their lifestyle and how they spend their time. Consider the groups, organizations, and clubs where these people belong and make it a habit of going there. Immerse yourself in what you desire and before long, you will move to the level you are seeking.

Action

Categorize the current influences in your life.

List your:

1. Disassociations (end the relationship)

2. Limited Associations (reduce time in the relationship)

3. Expanded Associations (invest more time in the relationship)

Look at your list of Expanded Associations and list some different ways you can mirror the success you want that you see in each of these people.

Daily Reflection

Before going to bed, reflect on your day's accomplishments. Bask in the positive effect they have had on your life. Embrace this feeling of happiness and warmth and visualize yourself move forward toward your Next Level of Living. Tomorrow is a new day, filled with new opportunities. As you close your eyes, picture the amazing day you will have tomorrow.

DAY 13
ACCEPT "WHAT IS"

Begin Each Day with Gratitude

In your companion Next Level Living Workbook record...

10 things I am grateful for today...

The comic strip, The Family Circus, features a feisty little character called Not Me who can be seen running from the scenes of various mischief committed by the kids in the family. Not Me is a visual representation of every guilty kid's favorite line when cornered by an angry adult demanding, "WHO DID THIS?" – "Not me!"

As you embark on today's lesson think about the role, if any, that Not Me – and his sidekick Not my Fault - have played in your life up to this point.

It's not my fault I don't have my dream job, it's not my fault I'm not happy, it's not my fault I don't have the life I desire... The question is: If not you, then who?

◆ *Next Level Lesson* ◆
Accepting What Is

Once you have identified "what is" in your life, it is important to go through your list and accept each item as your responsibility. This means making no excuses, laying no blame on others, and not indulging in denial. You created this life through your choices. All the people who may have influenced you did not force you to make the choices you have made to this point. Those choices were yours. As with every one of us, some of those choices were good and others produced what could be termed "learning experiences." Still you made those choices.

As I mentioned earlier, there are of course circumstances beyond your control, that is true, but you still choose how you react to those circumstances. In any event, 10% is really beyond your control, but 90% is in how you react to it.

No matter what your situation, there are choices that only you can make. If you start a sentence with, "But I can't," you are choosing to deny that you are responsible for your life. Until you accept that responsibility, you will not move forward.

It is fascinating that sometimes we truly cannot see how we have continued to blame others for our results. This is the time to dig deep and take a look at what you are doing, what is happening as a result and what you intend to do about it. Acknowledge and accept the now, because you created it. This is the day to declare "the buck stops here!"

Action

What are three things that you have a tendency to blame someone or something else for? Take a moment to think about how you might have blamed or perhaps are still blaming someone for your current situation. Write them down. Looking at these may be challenging and even a tad embarrassing, but remember this is part of your journey, and you are not expected to share your findings with anyone else. They are yours and yours alone. The knowledge you are discovering about who you are sets you up for growth and leads you up to the next level; the next level of being the best that you can be. The best you for YOU!!!

Daily Reflection

Before going to bed, review your gratitude list and reflect on the day's accomplishments. See the good in what you did today. Embrace it and move forward. Tomorrow is a new day, filled with new opportunities. As you close your eyes, picture the amazing day you will have tomorrow.

DAY 14
RECOGNIZE THAT YOU DESERVE A GREAT LIFE

Begin Each Day with Gratitude

In your companion Next Level Living Workbook record...

10 things I am grateful for today...

Try thinking of 10 things about yourself that you are grateful for.

◆ *Next Level Lesson* ◆
You Deserve a Great Life

I said before, that the "what is" is not a place from which to judge, it is a place to accept without excuses, blaming, or falling into entitlement thinking. Yes, everyone deserves a great life; however we cannot confuse this with a sense of entitlement. We each take our own journey from "what is" to "what can be."

As a young woman I made some decisions that for years I viewed as major mistakes. I felt that some of my family members and friends had a negative opinion of me because of some of the choices I made. I can look back now and understand that the circumstances, as unfortunate as they might have been, were a part of my journey that contributed to who I am today. When something negative would happen, I would hear that internal voice (self-talk) loud and clear. It would ask, "What did I really expect?" Like it was too much to hope to overcome the image I had of myself and to dream of a different life. I have realized that in order to step into the life I want – a phenomenal life – I have to believe I deserve it, and it is possible.

I know I'm not alone when I say that I bullied myself for years about things that happened in the past (that nasty negative "self-talk"). I am constantly meeting men and women who do the same thing. They assume that other people have a negative opinion of them (for whatever reason, their mind tricks them into believing this), and they keep their expectations of themselves low because of it. I can tell you from experience, you will only live up to your own expectations. If they are low, you will remain at that level with them. If they are high, and you partner that with positive "self-talk" and action, you will set and reach a higher level. Stay positive, and before you know it you will be ready to reach for another level.

Action

The way we see ourselves is part of our self-image. This image is formed over our entire lives and becomes deeply engrained in us. This perception influences how we interact with others. At times it can be difficult to really see yourself objectively, but often, if you look at the behaviors you are constantly repeating, you can uncover issues and then deal with them one by one.

What are the negative things you have been saying to yourself? Make a list of that negative "self-talk." Now write out what POSITVE "self-talk" you will replace those negative things with. POSITIVE "self-talk" is what will carry you forward.

Daily Reflection

Before going to bed, review your gratitude list, particularly the positive things about yourself and how they have contributed to who you are today. Look for the good in what you did, thought and learned today. Embrace it all and move forward. Tomorrow is a new day, filled with new opportunities. As you close your eyes, picture the amazing day you will have tomorrow.

DAY 15
KNOW YOURSELF AND OTHERS

Begin Each

Day with

Gratitude

In your companion Next Level Living Workbook record…

10 things I am grateful for today…

We know what we are, but know not what we may become.
- William Shakespeare

◆ *Next Level Lesson* ◆
Know Yourself and Others

Anyone who has ever tried to evaluate their life on their own knows that it's not easy. If you have ever looked at a pattern of behavior in your life and been completely dumbfounded as to why it keeps repeating, you know what I am talking about. Usually an outcome that keeps repeating indicates that there is an underlying cause. For example, if you've bailed yourself out of debt and made statements that you'd never let it happen again, then find yourself in the exact same boat, with overwhelming debt only a few months later. I also talk to many people who seem baffled at the relationships they get into. It is not unusual for them to say, "It's like I'm dating the same person over and over – I always think this one is different, but then they turn out to be the same."

A big part of taking your life to the next level includes understanding yourself and others at a deeper level. The more you can understand who you are and why you make the choices you do, you will understand when, where and how you might choose to adapt your behavior to bring about positive results in your life and relationships.

Behavioral Patterns

Behavioral patterns are indicators of where your strengths and weaknesses ("limitations" as I call them) lie, and they are often separated into four quadrants: Dominant, Influential, Steady, and Compliant. The study of these patterns dates back as far as Hippocrates (the great physician in 400 B.C.). Even then they used essentially the same four quadrants to analyze the health of people. The same is true of many of today's behavioral assessments.

One popular behavioral assessment that I use in my classes and business coaching practice is the DISC-People Keys report ("DISC" for short), which digs deeper into the four quadrants and establishes a base for improved communication and production levels. The DISC assessment provides insight into your preferred communication style. It also assesses how you function in a group and indicates what you truly value and what internally motivates you. If you have never taken an assessment like this before, it is a great starting point to evaluate your personality style.

This assessment will categorize you into one of four major personality styles that correlate with the previously mentioned quadrants: Dominant, Influential, Steady, and Compliant, and it gives you a score across each of the four preferences. Because most of us aren't just one personality type, it will allow you to see the combination of styles you possess and how to use them to your advantage.

Behavior of 4 Personality Styles

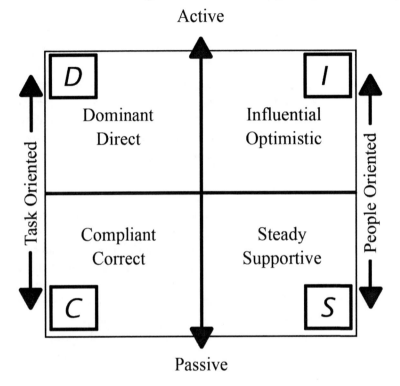

Active

D		I
Dominant Direct		Influential Optimistic
Compliant Correct		Steady Supportive
C		S

Task Oriented · People Oriented

Passive

Dominant/Driven

Individuals who are dominant tend to be the "doers." They are task oriented and outspoken. The positive aspects of this type of person are that they are independent, persistent, and direct. They can come across as fearless, busy and very energetic. On the negative side, they can be demanding and at times, tend to focus on their own goals rather than the wants and needs of others. This can often come across as bossy and egotistical depending on your perception of the situation. These are people who can undoubtedly get things done, but they sometimes steamroll over those around them in the process. Many CEOs, business owners, and professional athletes have this personality.

Influential/Optimistic

The term influential may be a little confusing, but this personality style is what you may think of as "creative" or the natural born "sales person." They are very social with many friends and tend to be optimistic and future-oriented. They focus on people rather than things or tasks. Quite honestly, these people are fun! Unfortunately, they may also tend to be poor time managers and if you have a friend or family member with this personality, then you have probably experienced them showing up late– including to their own wedding! Many artists, sales people and marketing/PR people tend to have this personality style.

Steady/Supportive

This type of person tends to stay in the background and is the solid foundation for others. They like keeping the peace, staying organized and finding solutions. They offer a strong shoulder to cry on and wise counsel. They tend to only have a few friends, but those relationships are strong. On the other hand, they also tend to be shy and avoid conflict. They don't like uncertainty and can get very stressed in times of change. Often people with this type of personality will take on jobs such as counseling, nursing, administrative, teaching or some other supportive or nurturing role.

Compliant/Correct

This type of person tends to be a perfectionist. They are critical thinkers and factor logic into all situations. They are very organized and follow rules to the letter. They are very private but have a few good friends. Sometimes this type of personality is described as cold or aloof. This is because they don't show emotion as freely as others do and are very private, not sharing things about their lives that most people don't think twice about sharing.

From these four types, we can make some broad generalizations to what personality type certain behaviors fall into:

	Dominant	Influential	Steady	Compliant/ Correct
Focus on other people		x	x	
Independent, perfectionist	x			x
Energetic and busy	x	x		
Tell rather than ask	x	x		
Imaginative, big-picture, future-focused	x	x		
Like stability and predict-ability			x	x
Like change	x	x		
Task oriented	x			x
Flexible to a changing world	x	x		

I realize that you may be thinking, so what? What do a four quadrant system from 400 B.C. and a big chart have to do with changing my behaviors and how I interact with others? It helps because it allows you to identify your own personality type, and then also identify the personalities of those around you. We all tend to attract people in our lives who balance us, which means that if you are a Dominant or Compliant personality then you may have a spouse or friend who is an Influential or Steady type of person. This balances you but also sets up the potential for conflict.

I have a client; we'll call her Marta for the sake of this story, who has a very dominant personality. She can get almost any project from point A to point B very efficiently and effectively. Her business partner, Susan, is quite different.

Susan is a bubbly creative and drives Marta crazy at times because she is so unorganized and never makes a meeting on time! But their partnership works. I asked Marta why their partnership works so well.

Years ago, I had another business partner in a venture that eventually failed. She had the same personality type as Susan and honestly, it drove me crazy.

I kept expecting my partner to change and be like me, and the fact that she couldn't resulted in tremendous stress and problems.

Eventually after the partnership dissolved, I realized that I missed her great creativity and positive energy. I had to take responsibility for the fact that I didn't know how to work with her personality – to take the good and let the bad go. We should have set up specific tasks and responsibilities drawing on our strengths.

When I started my current business, I realized I needed someone with that creative and positive mindset. My new partner, Susan, has that personality and while it can still drive me crazy when she shows up fifteen minutes late for everything,

I know that the creativity she brings to our business is vital. I'm committed to working hard to make this partnership work as well as possible. With the knowledge of DISC, we know how to communicate better to achieve the desired result.

Marta's balanced perspective shows the tremendous strides that can be made when you learn to work with the various personalities and capitalize on their good qualities while counterbalancing the possible negative aspects.

This one idea can improve your relationships and your life today, just by becoming aware and using some simple techniques to work with a particular personality type rather than against it.

Techniques

Dominant/Driven

If you are dealing with a dominant personality type in your life (and you are not one), rather than getting frustrated or intimidated, make an effort to understand what motivates them and where they are coming from. For example, when you discuss a particular issue, stick to the facts rather than focusing on the people involved. Talking about the people will be viewed as "drama," which this type tends to tune out. Keep in mind that dominant people are "bullet point" people. They want the facts without clutter and want to know how you can help them get from one point to the next with the fewest detours. They want to succeed, and they want to conquer, so show them how you can help them.

Influential/Optimistic

Influential people need to make a personal connection. They can't be rushed into the facts until they have chatted for a bit. They need encouragement to motivate them to complete tasks and set and meet clearly defined deadlines, rather than ultimatums. They need for you to listen to them, but your patience will be rewarded. Know up front that they may not be all that organized in follow through, and if you have that expectation, as Marta did with her first partner, then you will be disappointed. Approach this personality with caring and acceptance and an understanding of what will work.

Steady/Supportive

Steady people can be resistant to change. Any situation requiring them to change or alter their thinking must be approached with caution. They need for others to take a genuine interest in them as people and have little use for shallow relationships. They do not like to be rushed or forced to make decisions immediately. Patience is required as you allow them to adjust to the idea of change before committing to it, but it is the best way to get them on board with new ideas. These individuals respond well to those who take note of their accomplishments and abilities.

Compliant/Correct

Compliant people do not like surprises! Their world is one of habit and expectations and unexpected circumstances tend to be met with great resistance. In dealing with this type, you want to present facts and be prepared as they do not respond to someone shooting from the hip without concrete back up. If you have a conflict, be very specific and focus on the facts rather than the emotion of the event. With this type you must be persistent, diplomatic and patient.

If you need any help learning about behavioral patterns or want to take an assessment contact us at info@McLeanInternational.com, and we will be happy to help. The key is finding ways to learn more about yourself from an objective standpoint.

Once you have a good understanding of your behavioral characteristics, you can then begin to make the changes in your behavior and communication style with others. This is yet another step toward your Next Level of Living as well as a leap toward experiencing better overall outcomes in your life. This knowledge is a huge asset in accepting others for who they are with their strengths and weaknesses, while acknowledging who you are!

Action

Knowing yourself better means getting clear about your strengths and struggles. I always like to tell my clients to develop their strengths and manage their weaknesses. Some personal development coaches may say that you should only focus on your strengths because thinking about your weaknesses attracts more of that behavior into your life, but this is only partially true. What I'm talking about is identifying and recognizing the problems, so you can then focus on specific solutions that improve your life. You aren't going to dwell on the problems, you are going to focus on the solutions, but you will never find those solutions if you don't create the awareness of the issues that are holding your back.

Spend some time now writing down your three greatest strengths and three greatest weaknesses. What will you do to develop those strengths? What will you do to manage your weaknesses?

Daily Reflection

Before going to bed, review your gratitude list and reflect on the day's accomplishments and all the knowledge about understanding yourself and others that you have gained today. Look for the good in your thoughts, words, actions and results. Embrace it all and visualize yourself moving forward to your next level. Tomorrow is a new day, filled with new opportunities. As you close your eyes, picture the amazing day you will have tomorrow.

DAY 16
SEE HOW YOU ARE MULTI-FACETED

Begin Each Day with Gratitude

In your companion Next Level Living Workbook, record…

10 things I am grateful for today…

"Where do you see yourself in five years?" is a popular job interview question, but how many of us actually take it to heart and ask it about all areas of our lives, from work to relationships to our spiritual path? Today, on day 16 of your journey, you will have that opportunity and the tools you need to visualize your next level life.

◆ *Next Level Lesson* ◆
We Are Multi-Faceted

Are you a Rock Star? A Star? Only a Rock? I believe that each of us is a rock, but the most beautiful rock imaginable. A diamond! Just as a diamond has many facets to the stone, so it is with our lives. We have many different angles we can see ourselves from and many different areas that make up who we are. In order to hold that "sparkle," we need to be fully engaged in each area of our lives. There are of course times in everyone's life when certain facets are skimmed over and not really addressed. It really depends on where you are in your life. It is more important to create the awareness that each of these facets is necessary to become fully engaged and happy in our lives.

In my Next Level Living classes, I teach students to focus on eight specific facets of their lives. On Day 11 you first encountered these facets and started to look at and consider "What is" true about each one: Personal Growth, Health, Relationship, Financial, Business/Career/School, Spiritual, Recreation, and Community.

As you consider your own life and the diamond you are, I want you to remember that things can be different. You can take your life to the next level.

Now that you have completed your "What Is" analysis, you have a base to work from. Next ask yourself, "When you get to where you are going in your life, where will that be?" Consider this for the next five years, ten years, and even twenty years.

There are really two questions to ask yourself:

1) "If you keep going in the same direction you are heading right now and keep doing the same things over and over the same way, what will your life look like? Not only in terms of your career and finances, but what kind of person will you be?"

2) "Where do you want to be in five years, ten years, and twenty years from now?"

It has been my experience that most people do not spend much time contemplating these ideas, but as Henry David Thoreau once said, "In the long run, we only hit what we aim at." You must be clear about where you are aiming in order to arrive where you want to be.

Action

What would you like the following facets of your life to look like in 5 years, 10 years, and 20 years?

1. Personal Growth

2. Health

3. Relationships

4. Financial

5. Business/Career/School

6. Spiritual

7. Recreation

8. Community

Daily Reflection

Before going to bed, review your gratitude list and reflect on your accomplishments and knowledge gained today. See the steps you've taken toward your future goals in all facets of your life. Acknowledge all the good in what you did today. Embrace it and move forward. Tomorrow is a new day, filled with new opportunities. As you close your eyes, picture the amazing day you will have tomorrow.

JEWELS FOR THE JOURNEY
THE POWER OF WORDS

We are now moving into days on your Next Level Living journey that feature the unique power words have to change your thoughts, perceptions and intentions about life. Upcoming lessons and exercises will focus on how the words you choose to articulate your goals can make all the difference in how successfully and how quickly you achieve those goals.

Words can have tremendous power. They can uplift and inspire, and they can also tear down and hurt us. The most harmful words and phrases are those that we tell ourselves about ourselves. We know all our past failures and all our shortcomings. We can also be our own worst critic. The vast majority of the time, the only thing standing between you and what you want are the words and ideas you tell yourself. No one can know your potential or what you can accomplish, and this includes you. You have no idea how far you can go in life until you try, but often the harsh words we use internally tear ourselves down and prevent us from doing anything more than what we are doing right now. Your words should not be your worst enemy. They should be your best friend, there to move you forward toward your goals.

Now, it's time to move forward to the next day of your Next Level journey!

DAY 17
CREATE SMART GOALS

Begin Each Day with Gratitude

In your companion Next Level Living Workbook, record…

10 things I am grateful for today…

Have you ever noticed how as kids, we're constantly setting goals – play this new game after school, do or get this on my birthday, finish building this fort by summer, etc.? So why then as adults, does the word "goal" suddenly become a daunting, insurmountable word? In my opinion it's because at some point, we took the fun out of the fun stuff. As you read today's lesson, I want you to keep reminding yourself – the fun stuff is fun!

◆ *Next Level Lesson* ◆
SMART Goals and The Why behind them

Now that you have cast your vision for what you want to see happen in the next several years, it is time to back up just a bit and create specific goals in each area.

Goal setting is something everyone knows is helpful but few people take the time to actually do it. Although statistics show you are far more likely to reach your goals just by writing them down, still less than 10% of the population does so. Note: if you are the type of person who does not like the concept of "goals" and "goal setting," replace that term throughout the rest of this book with one that resonates with you better. You might prefer "changes" or "dreams." Don't let yourself get stopped from making progress in life because you don't like a certain verbiage.

There are SMART cars and SMART phones but what about the goals we set for ourselves that have the power to help us ascend from level to level in life? Today we are going to start by writing out at least two specific goals you would like to see accomplished in the next 12 months for each facet of life. As you are creating goals, keep in mind a powerful goal is one that is SMART. That is Specific, Measurable, Attainable, Realistic and Time-limited.

So if you first take on the financial facet of your life, you would focus on specific financial goals that will improve your personal financial position. This is more than just saying something like, "I want more money." While this may certainly be your goal, it has to be specific. So you might say, "I will invest an additional $15,000 into my savings account by December 31st." or "I will actively look for a higher paying job on May 1st." This gives you something very concrete that will allow you to track and monitor your progress. You also want to keep all your goals measurable, attainable, realistic and time-limited.

Paige and Katie, both 16 years old and friends since 2006, were on the same path, without even realizing it. Actively involved in athletics, studying and getting A's just wasn't enough, they were both ready to reach loftier goals.

On a sunny afternoon in 2008 the girls realized they had each decided to graduate from high school a year early. At first it was a bit of a joke, but the more they allowed themselves to dream of starting college in the fall, the more they began to get attached to the idea. With excitement and determination, they supported each other in their goal of walking across the stage on June 4, 2008 receiving their High School Diplomas a year earlier than scheduled.

The process of meeting with teachers, counselors, and the principal, as well as taking online classes, missing out on many social events, and scheduling extra homework time was very specific and purposeful for them in getting the needed credits to graduate early.

It wasn't easy for these girls, but they pushed forward by keeping their eye on the prize and being willing to sacrifice short term enjoyment to meet a long term goal.

Their goal to graduate early was translated into several SMART (Specific, Measurable, Attainable, Realistic and Time-limited) goals including:

◆ Completing four needed credits before May 2008.

◆ Getting approval from each school authority before the school year began.

◆ And walking across the stage to graduate on June 4, 2008.

Although these goals were lofty and stretching, they were doable based on all aspects of their past experience and abilities, and those around them agreed. When June 4th came, I am proud to say Paige, my youngest daughter, and her best friend, Katie, both graduated at age 17 ready to begin their higher education in medicine and law respectively.

The Why

In addition to creating SMART goals it is also important to understand your own motives around each goal. You want to be sure to consider and capture "the why" for each goal you have. For Paige and Katie, it was to get started studying what they were really interested in sooner and to leave behind the less challenging days of high school.

How about you? "Why" is it important for you to reach your goals? Knowing this reminds you that each goal is connected to your larger motivations and values in life. Without a strong and compelling "why," the motivation required to complete or achieve your goals will soon fade away.

Action

While considering each facet in your life, set two SMART goals per facet. These goals should reflect what you want to see happen in the next year in each area. As you go through your list of goals, consider "the why" for each one. "Why" are they each important to you and "why" do you want to accomplish them? Don't skip this step in the process. This is a critical part to really giving your goals traction. As you capture your goals on this one list, it becomes your Master List of Goals for the year.

Daily Reflection

Before going to bed, review your gratitude list and reflect on the day's accomplishments. Look for the good in what you did today. Embrace it and see yourself moving forward toward your SMART Goals. Tomorrow is a new day, filled with new opportunities. Your Next Level of Living is closer than you think! As you close your eyes, picture the amazing day you will have tomorrow.

DAY 18
UNCOVER THE FIVE POWER QUESTIONS

Begin Each Day with Gratitude

Begin the Day with Gratitude:

In your companion Next Level Living Workbook, record...

10 things I am grateful for today...

*There are no foolish questions, and no man becomes a
fool until he has stopped asking questions.*
-Charles Proteus Steinmetz

◆ *Next Level Lesson* ◆
The Five Power Questions

You have taken the time to create goals for all the facets of your life, so you will surely have a lot of goals! I've seen many people just sit and stare at their lists of goals like a deer in the headlights, because they are overwhelmed and have no idea where to start. Obviously, we need a way to prioritize these lists. One of the best ways I've found is by asking a few additional questions, which will make it very clear which of your goals should be your priorities. We will discuss each question here and then give you the opportunity to answer them all in your Action for the day.

1. What personal needs do I have that, when fulfilled, will make me a happier and better person?

This question gets to the heart of what you need to be happy. Happiness as a concept is hard to define and different for everyone. In fact, for many of us it is a constantly evolving idea. What made us happy a few years ago won't necessarily make us happy today. Because you have already filled out the lists of goals for the various areas of your life, you have a much better start at figuring out what really feeds into your own concept of happiness.

2. What have I always wanted to do but have been afraid to attempt?

Sometimes, when people fill out the goal sheets for the various areas of their life, they self-edit along the way. This means they allow their fears to dictate what does or does not appear in their goals. But you can't allow your old fears or ideas to stand in the way of those things you have always wanted to try. Have you ever wanted to take flying lessons, go to Africa, ride a camel in Egypt, or skydive? It doesn't necessarily have to be life threatening or major thrill seeking, but we all have those ideas that we have set aside as impractical, dangerous, or beyond our abilities. Adding some of these goals into your priority list adds excitement. Your goal may be as simple as going on a cruise if you've never been on one. Really consider those things that pop into your mind that you have pushed aside. Now add them to your list.

3. What do I enjoy doing most in my life and if money was no object I would do full time?

This is what you actually enjoy, not what you are obligated to do or what others think you should enjoy. What do you love to do that you would do for hours on end if you could? For some people this isn't what they spend much time doing in the course of their daily lives. It's a hobby or something they only get to do on occasion. Figure out what that is for you and find those goals on your list that support that enjoyment.

4. When I have reached the end of my life, what do I want to look back and feel good about? What do I want to be remembered for?

These questions really allow you to put things into perspective. Reflect back on the eight facets of your life to determine briefly what you want to feel good about when your life comes to an end. Maybe it is having wonderful relationships with family and friends, committing your life to serving your spiritual beliefs, building a highly successful international business, taking great care of your health, or adding a new wing to your local hospital. Whatever it is for you, remember the important thing is to honor yourself. This is your life and as you close your eyes before you leave this world, what thoughts will you be thinking – ones of regret or ones of gratitude for a life well lived?

5. If I only had six months to live, how would I spend my time? Where would I go? What would I do? Who would I want to spend time with?

Time is a thief, and it steals some of life's great experiences if we let it. We can put off accomplishing some of our important goals because we are so busy taking care of the urgent issues in our lives. This can lead us to never accomplish what really matters. Thinking within the context of an abbreviated timeframe, shines a spotlight on the vital goals while dimming the excitement of less significant ideas.

I cannot encourage you enough to schedule time in your calendar to think about and more importantly write down what you would truly do within those six months. For some it might be to take the vacation of their dreams, while others might want to visit family and friends, and others might want to do something totally outlandish. It doesn't matter!! This is your life. Create your list with no strings attached and create your plan.

Action

Take some time to answer each of the questions for yourself:

1. What personal needs do I have that, when fulfilled, will make me a happier and better person?

2. What have I always wanted to do but have been afraid to attempt?

3. What do I enjoy doing most in my life, and if money was no object I would do full time?

4. When I have reached the end of my life, what do I want to look back and feel good about? What do I want to be remembered for?

5. If I only had six months to live, how would I spend my time? Where would I go? What would I do? Who would I want to spend time with?

Use these questions to help you get clear about your own priorities.

Daily Reflection

Before going to bed, review your gratitude list and reflect on the day's accomplishments. Know that even after you go to sleep tonight, your brain will continue to seek answers to the questions you put into play today. Embrace this forward progress and celebrate where you are on your journey to the next level. Tomorrow is a new day, filled with new opportunities. As you close your eyes, picture the amazing day you will have tomorrow.

DAY 19
SET YOUR TOP 6 GOALS

Begin Each Day with Gratitude

In your companion Next Level Living Workbook, record…

10 things I am grateful for today…

> *Get busy livin', or get busy dyin'*
> *-The Bucket List*

◆ *Next Level Lesson* ◆
Set Your Top 6 Goals

A few years ago there was a movie starring Jack Nicholson and Morgan Freeman called The Bucket List. The idea of a "bucket list" is to make a list of all the things you want to accomplish before you die, and then complete them and cross them off one at a time. Both characters were diagnosed with cancer and the abbreviated time frame focused their efforts on doing some of the things in their lives they'd never made time to do. The most interesting thing about these two individuals was that they lived, as most of us do, with a mindset of just getting through their days and not giving a second thought to what is really important, until they were forced to face the harsh reality of pending death.

My favorite line from the movie is, "Get busy livin', or get busy dyin'." That is how we should approach our list of goals each day. We can make the most of the time we have and create the best life possible, or we can waste our years by just "getting by." The choice is ours.

Looking at your Master List of Goals, it may feel a little overwhelming, and you may doubt that you can accomplish them all. But remember the power of your mind and the sequence of events that take place with your thinking.

Thoughts → Images → Emotions → Actions → Results

Keep reminding yourself that how you are thinking about your goals will impact your ability to accomplish them. Confidence is required to go out and achieve them.

Confidence is an interesting emotion. Think of something you have done numerous times and that you feel totally comfortable doing again. It may be taking a trip and going through the exercise of planning it, booking the flight, getting to the airport, checking in, going through security and boarding the airplane. For some people this is a daunting exercise, while others who have done it numerous times are totally confident in the process, because they have done it over and over again. The same is true for cooking for a group or singing in front of people. Whatever the activity is, when a person feels confident about what they are about to encounter, they approach it with a positive mindset therefore their actions are geared towards positivity and guess what happens? The event occurs without a hitch!!

Inner confidence breeds quicker action. Whereas when you are hesitant you don't act quickly and tread carefully, leading you to spin your wheels – walking in place. As you overcome difficulties you face, you inevitably build the confidence you will need to start walking forward again, pushing on toward your big goals.

Action

Your next step is to pare down your Master List of Goals to your Top 6 Goals. What are the goals that you really, really want and know must be started TODAY in order to be achieved? Working with your Top 6 Goals will bring your time, energy and financial resources into great focus – like a laser beam instead of a flood light. A laser beam gathers all its power and focuses it onto one point. The result is when it strikes an object, it has such intensity behind it that it can cut or melt almost anything instantly.

In contrast, a flood light covers a broad area with its light but has little heat intensity and is not capable of cutting or melting as a result. Keep this in mind when you are working on your goals. The higher level of intensity will lead to more powerful results. Whereas using the flood light approach of spreading yourself over a wide area, leads to less effective results. Yes it may use less energy, but it also produces much weaker results.

Now to get your efforts focused. What are your Top 6 Goals?

Daily Reflection

Before going to bed, review your gratitude list and reflect on the day's accomplishments – what fun! Even as you read this, those accomplishments are moving you one step closer toward your goals. Look for the good in what you did today. Embrace it and move forward. Tomorrow is a new day, filled with new opportunities. As you close your eyes tonight, picture the amazing day you will have tomorrow.

DAY 20
DETERMINE WHERE THE RUBBER MEETS THE ROAD

Begin Each

Day with

Gratitude

In your companion Next Level Living Workbook, record...

10 things I am grateful for today...

Taken literally, "Where the Rubber Meets the Road" means when the rubber on car tires makes contact with the pavement and the car is set in motion. Figuratively, it refers to the moment of truth – when you find out what you're made of by taking action.

◆ *Next Level Lesson* ◆
Where the Rubber Meets the Road

As I mentioned before, you can't pluck a diamond out of the ground and with a quick wipe of a cloth expect it to be brilliant and shiny. Diamond cutting and polishing requires anywhere from several hours to several months to complete. During this process, a diamond will lose on average half of its original weight. That's commitment! Repetition is the key to success; the more reps the better the results. Look at the great Wayne Gretzky. This former professional hockey player (who happens to be a fellow Canadian) is considered "the greatest hockey player in history." Just like many other successful athletes, his work ethic and commitment to practice was insurmountable. The key to Wayne's success, one that we can all learn from, is to take action. One of Wayne's quotes sums it up. "Procrastination is one of the most common and deadliest of diseases and its toll on success and happiness is heavy." Give yourself the gift of action. You will feel better for it and ultimately so will others around you.

Procrastination is not your friend. It is one of the tricksters keeping you trapped in that dark basement and making you believe you have no other options. If you're thinking that you will start working toward your goals after the holidays, on your birthday, or after this or that happens, you are just deluding yourself. Every day that goes by without your taking action is a day wasted. You won't get it back, and you don't get to try again. The day is gone forever. So start today and plug into the process. Being focused on a goal means you take the necessary steps, whatever those may be, to achieve it.

Action

For each goal on your Top 6 Goals List document the action steps necessary over the next year to accomplish it. Don't be afraid to map-out even the smallest steps you'll have to take. Getting clear about all the actions needed will give you a game plan to achieve your goal.

Daily Reflection

Before going to bed, review your gratitude list and reflect on the action you took today. Look for the good, celebrate it and continue moving forward on your journey. Tomorrow is a new day, filled with new opportunities. As you close your eyes, picture the amazing day you will have tomorrow.

Jewels for
the Journey
Moving Forward

The most interesting aspect of goal setting exercises, like the one you just completed, is it allows your mind to move forward. Now that you have opened up and allowed yourself to really dream, your life has undoubtedly already changed because your perspective has been altered.

As you continue on the path toward your Next Level of Living each day, your world as you know it expands. Not because it just happened out of the blue, but because you just noticed. We all go through life with blinders on only knowing what we experience every day. But once in a while, we allow ourselves to really dream of a different life and imagine a new way to exist - this is the real secret to creating a new life. This is Next Level Living.

As with almost everything in life, there are no short cuts to reaching the next level. If you are merely reading this without taking Action along the way, you are cheating yourself out of a powerful phase of self-discovery.

I'll be the first to admit that introspection can be very hard sometimes, especially if you don't like what you see. But it is completely necessary and worth the temporary discomfort. So if you have not been working through the exercises, now is the time to go back and walk through each of them. By doing so, you will see change in your life.

Planning and thinking about where you want to go in life is never a waste of time. Schedule a specific amount of time, I suggest 30 minutes to an hour, to go back and complete any incomplete Actions or exercises. If you completed everything up to this point – fantastic! Your next level is in sight.

DAY 21
SEEK FEEDBACK AND EVALUATIONS

Begin Each

Day with

Gratitude

In your companion Next Level Living Workbook, record...

10 things I am grateful for today ...

Today, think about feedback you have received from others that has helped you in life

Champions know that success is inevitable; that there is no such thing as failure, only feedback. They know that the best way to forecast the future is to create it.

-Michael J. Gelb

◆ *Next Level Lesson* ◆
Feedback and Evaluation

In order to achieve your goals, you will need to be flexible in your goal setting. This does not mean giving yourself permission to fall back into an old rut. This means using creativity to overcome obstacles and also being willing to listen to feedback from others.

This will help you fine-tune your goals and action steps as you go.

Feedback is important because no matter how well you've researched or planned, there may be some areas that you've overlooked or are unaware of. And the reality is that you don't know what you don't know. Also from time to time, you may lose your perspective and be unable to correctly assess your own efforts. At those times a wise or experienced friend, family member, business associate, or life coach can help you get back on track.

Regularly evaluating your progress can help you assess how you are progressing and also help you course correct if necessary. Stepping back and evaluating your progress should help you stay focused and mindful of your goals and where you want to go from here. This evaluation loop will not only help you get clear about where you are currently but will also give you some clear actions to start or stop in order to achieve success.

Action

List three people you could share your goals with. Bring them into the process and allow them to support you during your journey. Your list of "support beams" on Day 6 should provide you with some possible people to choose from.

Also consider how often you would like to evaluate your progress. Planning for these evaluations now, with those listed above, will ensure they happen. Go ahead and put them on your calendar.

During each evaluation ask yourself and discuss with those supporting you:

◆ What is working?

◆ What is not working?

◆ What changes are needed to get better results?

Daily Reflection

Before going to bed, review the list of feedback you wrote earlier today and realize that it is meant to help you grow and succeed in your journey to the next level. Reflect on the day's accomplishments. Look for the good in it, embrace it and move forward. Tomorrow is a new day, filled with new opportunities. As you close your eyes, picture the amazing day you will have tomorrow.

DAY 22
STICK TO YOUR PLAN

Begin Each Day with Gratitude

In your companion Next Level Living Workbook, record...

10 things I am grateful for today...

As we come to the end of section two, in which you have begun to chart your course to the next level, this is an excellent time to skim through all your gratitude lists so far. Do you see any common themes and patterns in the things, people and circumstances for which you are grateful?

◆ *Next Level Lesson* ◆
Stick to your Plan

Stick to your plan and avoid the traps that can occur along the way. You will undoubtedly find that as you are working on your goals, and moving through your thinking and planning processes, obstacles will pop up. Cement the idea in your mind now, that no obstacle, no matter how big, has the power to keep you from moving forward. Resolve to get either around, over or under the obstacles you are faced with. Be solution focused and stick to your ultimate plan. It is similar to charting a road trip for your vacation and then arriving at a detour. You decide to take the detour, continuing on with your vacation. A person doesn't stop, turn around go back home and cancel their vacation because of one little detour.

Build on what you have. Learn from each lesson as you make consistent progress. One of Newton's laws of motion is that "An object in motion stays in motion, while an object at rest stays at rest." The same is true of the human mind. If you feel in control and that you are making progress, then it is easier to keep going. However, if you feel out of control, stuck and allow yourself to stop, it takes even more effort to get started again than when you initially began your journey.

Action

List three things that help you "KEEP going." And three things that help you "GET going again" when you feel stuck.

Daily Reflection

Before going to bed, reflect on your accomplishments today. Look for the collective good, embrace it and move forward. Tomorrow is a new day, filled with new opportunities. As you close your eyes on this, day 22 of your journey, picture the amazing day you will have tomorrow.

REVIEW

Congratulations you have reached your second checkpoint!!! Let's review how far you have come on your journey in this section...

You have...

◆ Dug deep into "What is" your current situation.

◆ Categorized influences in your life as ....Disassociations, Limited Associations or Expanded Associations.

◆ Documented where you have been blaming or are still blaming others.

◆ Replaced your Negative self-talk with Positive self-talk.

◆ Gained knowledge on your strengths and weaknesses.

◆ Created a vision for what you would like your life to be like in 5, 10 and 20 years.

◆ Created two SMART goals for each of the 8 facets of your life – resulting in your Master Goals List.

◆ Become clear about "The Why" behind each goal.

◆ Asked yourself the 5 Power Questions allowing them to help you prioritize your Top 6 Goals.

◆ Clearly articulated action steps for each Top Goal.

◆ Created a feedback and evaluation cycle.

◆ Documented what "keeps you going" and "what gets you going" again.

Wow, you have achieved quite a lot and in a relatively short period of time too! As you look at the list, if you see exercises that you have not completed along the way, I would encourage you to take a little time and go back and complete them now. You will only get out of this process as much as you put into it, and my hope for you is that you are already seeing significant results in your journey to the next level. Give yourself a pat on the back and stick with it!

SECTION THREE
SUPPORT YOUR JOURNEY WITH AFFIRMATIONS AND VISUALIZATIONS

Day 23 ◆ Write Affirmations that Create Action

Day 24 ◆ Bring Life to Your Goals

Day 25 ◆ Explore Different Types of Vision Boards

Day 26 ◆ Keep Pressing On

Day 27 ◆ Be Persistently Perseverant

Day 28 ◆ Gain Satisfaction

Day 29 ◆ Reach for Your Rope of Hope

Review

DAY 23
WRITE AFFIRMATIONS THAT CREATE ACTION

Begin Each

Day with

Gratitude

In your companion Next Level Living Workbook, record...

10 things I am grateful for today...

Does the word "Write" threaten to trigger a case of writer's block in you before you even write a single word? Well guess what, even though this is the first day where the word "write" is the title of the day, you have been writing constantly throughout your journey so far. Between your daily gratitude lists and all your action exercises, you might even have enough for your own book by now!

◆ *Next Level Lesson* ◆
Write Affirmations that Create Action

Our subconscious mind determines who we become, what we achieve, and what we acquire. It can help us reach great heights or keep us in the same rut we've known for years. The good news is that we have the power to purposefully plant the seeds for growth and achievement in our subconscious mind. In order to make this change, we must bombard our subconscious with the new thoughts and images of what we desire. Whether it is a larger bank account, a trim and healthy body, more meaningful relationships, the perfect business, memorable vacations, or a stronger spiritual path, we plant thoughts in our mind as if we have already completed our goals and are now living the life we want. This is called positive affirmation, and it works as if we are playing a movie on the screen of our mind that shows the end result we will achieve.

Affirmations serve two purposes. First, they allow us to convince ourselves of what is possible, and that we can achieve those things we desire. Second, they replace or squeeze out the old, negative thoughts that are holding us back. It is much like healthy grass squeezing out the dandelions in your yard. The more positive ideas that you purposely focus on, the fewer negative thoughts that can get through and thus fewer negative events are likely to occur in your life.

It may seem silly to think that you have to convince yourself of anything, but if you consider how often during the course of a day you catch yourself allowing a negative idea to flutter across your mind, you can see how challenging it can be to be positive and to work toward your goals, especially if you are constantly telling yourself you can't do it. I like to imagine the subconscious as a big bucket, and your goals are like water filling that bucket. Now if you imagine that your negative thoughts are small holes in the bottom of the bucket, you can guess that the more holes there are, the less likely that the bucket will ever fill up no matter how much water you pour in. As you work on creating more positive thoughts through affirmations, you plug those holes, and before long your goals are being reached more easily and quickly.

Our thoughts become images, and those images incite emotions. When the emotions are strong enough, we take action or change our behavior, and this produces our results.

Thoughts → Images → Emotions → Actions → Results

Emotions help us connect with what we want and create an expectation that we will achieve it. It is not a want or wish, but an inevitable conclusion.

6 Steps to Valuable Affirmations

In order to create valuable positive affirmations, use the following language:

1. **The present tense.** An affirmation is not a wish or hope, but an expectation of the inevitable. Therefore the words "I am" are the most powerful words in creating effective affirmations. When the subconscious mind hears the words "I am," it interprets them as an order - a directive to make it happen. Your affirmation should describe what you want as though you already have it or as though you have accomplished the goal.

Incorrect: I want to buy a new Lexus GX470.

Correct: I am enjoying driving my new white Lexus GX470.

2. **Positive statements.** It is important to be very clear on what you want rather than focusing on what you don't want. The subconscious mind does not hear the word "don't." This means that the statement "I don't eat cake" is heard as "eat cake".

The mind thinks in pictures, so the words "I don't eat cake" elicit a picture of eating cake! No wonder it is so hard for people to stay on a diet, when their mind is constantly focused on what they don't want to eat. The same is also true with finances or relationships. If we focus on what we don't want, that's what we get.

Incorrect: I am not overdrawn in my bank account anymore.

Correct: I am feeling super successful with more than enough funds in my bank account every month.

3. **Short and specific statements**. Your affirmation must be short enough to be easily memorized and use very specific rather than general wording. Specificity is extremely important so that the goal is easily measurable, and you readily know when it is achieved. If your affirmation is "I am making more money than last year," technically $1 is more money, but is that really what you wanted? Probably not. So you would instead have an affirmation that perhaps says "I am thrilled with the fact that my salary has more than doubled in the past year."

Incorrect: I am going to lose weight.

Correct: I am feeling proud and celebrating that I am at my ideal weight of 125 lbs.

4. **Action words create power**. By incorporating a strong action word ending in "ing" the image in your mind will receive the command of doing it right now. Emotion drives motivation, therefore add one dynamic emotional or feeling word such as enthusiastic, triumphant, proudly, joyfully, enjoying, happily, peacefully, delighted and celebrating.

Incorrect: I am going to run a marathon.

Correct: I am thrilled now that I am crossing the finish line of my first marathon.

5. **Personal Power**. Your affirmations are about you and not created for others. They are to describe your behavior and not the behavior or desires of others. You can't force others to change, you can only change yourself. Your affirmations should not get tangled up with what others expect from you or what you expect from them. They are all about you and you alone.

Incorrect: I am happy my child is now getting great grades.

Correct: I am feeling pleased now that I have arranged private tutoring for my child.

6. **Open Ended and Limitless.** When you become clear and specific on what you desire, add the words "or something better" to your affirmations. Sometimes, we limit what we receive as a result of our experiences, exposure or ego. By allowing your affirmations to be open ended and limitless, you are allowing more good to flow to you, and often it appears in ways we could have never predicted. So leave yourself open to receive these gifts.

Incorrect: I am feeling triumphant now that I own a three bedroom cottage on Wonder Lake.

Correct: I am feeling triumphant now that I own a three bedroom cottage on Wonder Lake – or something even better.

You can have fun creating your own personal affirmations.

Expanding Your Affirmations

Some people have difficulty getting started with affirmations, especially if they have carried a negative mindset for years. In order to help you in the process of developing your own affirmations, here is a list of examples:

Note: A more extensive list of affirmations is in Appendix C at the back of the book.

Positive Affirmations:

◆ I am feeling the power of a healthy body and mind.

◆ I am celebrating the happy relationships I have with my family, friends and business associates.

◆ I am participating in a daily quiet time reflecting, praying and visualizing.

◆ I am proud that I am eating fruits, vegetables, carbohydrates, and protein in balance.

◆ I am delighted my home is completely decorated and renovated to my desire.

◆ I am effectively listening to what others have to say with genuine interest and respect.

It is very important that you say your affirmations to yourself a minimum of three times each day. This is especially true in the early weeks and months, because you are trying to replace old thought patterns. It's very much like pulling weeds the second you yank one out another pops up. However, persistence pays off, and as you bombard your mind with these positive thoughts on a regular basis, you will also become much more aware of the negative words and thoughts you are leaving behind and replacing with positive ones. This will help you stop them before they take root in your mind again.

Supporting Your Affirmations

Having all your affirmations in a single document on your computer can be very helpful. This allows you to have a single record of your affirmations to print out and place copies in different locations (office, car, briefcase, kitchen, etc.). You should also consider writing them on 3 x 5 cards and carrying them with you at all times. That way if you are waiting for a meeting, in the doctor's office or even in line at the supermarket you have the opportunity to read these powerful, positive statements. Make your down time productive time! Many people also record their affirmations in an endless loop on an MP3 player, iPod, or other device and listen to them while exercising, driving or going to sleep at night. Another idea is to set your affirmations as your screen saver so that throughout the day you see those positive words repeatedly while sitting at your desk.

I encourage you to be creative and look for all the opportunities to replace your habitual negative thoughts with positive ones. The more you can do this, the faster you will see results and meet your goals.

Action

Using your Top 6 Goals, create an affirmation for each of them. I highly encourage you to date the work you are doing. You will find revisiting it in a couple of months and even years, to see what you wrote, enlightening and encouraging. It is a witness of where you were and how you have progressed.

There are two types of affirmations. 1) Those directly associated with a specific goal and 2) Those that help position your thinking and help you connect to certain emotions and mindsets. They bring everything together in a way that is more like a statement than an affirmation. I call these Connector Affirmations. An example would be, "I actively embrace the opportunities that come with change." Or "I deeply appreciate and accept myself just the way I am." (For more examples of Connector Affirmations see Appendix D.) These are also very powerful tools for you to be aware of. In addition to the affirmations you've already written, create one Connector Affirmation as well.

This is another reminder that how we talk to ourselves sends a strong message to our "internal self," which directly impacts the results we get. Throughout the day, observe how you talk to yourself about yourself. When you catch yourself thinking something negative or less than desirable about yourself, STOP right there, and speak positive words which help to change the image on the screen of your mind to a new channel: the new, positive YOU channel. Practice some kindness toward yourself by giving yourself permission to release the mistakes or regrets you have from the past and take the next step up the stairs, moving in the direction of your goals. Focus on today and what you can accomplish. Give yourself a little pep talk that you can do it!

Daily Reflection

Before going to bed, review your gratitude list and reflect on the day's accomplishments. Look for the good in what you did and celebrate the powerful affirmations that you put into words today. Embrace your success and continue moving forward toward your next level. Tomorrow is a new day, filled with new opportunities. As you close your eyes, picture the amazing day you will have tomorrow.

DAY 24
BRING LIFE TO YOUR GOALS

Begin Each

Day with

Gratitude

In your companion Next Level Living Workbook, record...

10 things I am grateful for today...

The vision that you glorify in your mind, the ideal that you enthrone in your heart, this you will build your life by, and this you will become.

-Source Unknown

◆ *Next Level Lesson* ◆
Bringing Life to Your Goals

The emotional connection we have when visualizing our achievements is wonderfully uplifting, but it can be very hard to hold these pictures firmly in our minds as the day grinds on. This challenge is easily overcome with what is known as a vision board. A vision board is a physical representation of your goals. It might have photos of places you want to visit, the salary you want to earn, the house you want to live in, or the relationship you want to have; essentially those things that you most desire.

The idea is that you have something visual in front of you every single day that shows you at a glance what you want and dream of. It helps you stay plugged into the process of achieving those things, which ultimately determines what your next level will look like and the goals you are gravitating towards.

Thoughts and physical images connect with your emotions which drives motivation. Motivation causes action and action yields results. A vision board is a very positive and affirming tool, and it allows you to easily track your progress. As goals are met, you replace those images with new ones.

There is no "right" way to create your board; however the first step is to think of what types of pictures you'll need to collect to represent your goals.

A great example confirming the power of both a vision board and affirmations is my own. I'm sure you noticed that a couple of the example affirmations in yesterday's lesson concerned a white Lexus GX470. This was taken straight from my own affirmations and vision board.

Several years ago, my family would sometimes stop at the local Lexus dealership on our way home from church. That's when I first saw this beautiful white Lexus, and I instantly connected with it. I just didn't see how we could afford that kind of car at that point in our lives. But I still took a brochure home, cut out the picture and added it to my vision board. And there it stayed for five years. Yes, five years!

Not long after we moved to the Reno/Lake Tahoe area, we talked about me getting a new car. Since I was driving our children here and there on the snow and at times in the mountains, it made sense. Even at that point, I didn't think getting a GX470 was going to happen. Then on Christmas day, we were all sitting around the tree opening our packages and being so grateful for our gifts. As my gift, my children and husband sent me on a treasure hunt. They had hidden little clues all around the house, until the last clue was the car key taped on the back of the door leading to the garage.

Now I recognized the Lexus logo immediately and wondered if the car I'd visualized for more than five years could really be sitting in the garage. As I opened the door, there it was – a beautiful, brand-new, white Lexus GX470! It had a huge red bow on top, just like you see in commercials.

Something really uncanny is that I later found out that my husband was also negotiating on a BMW. He felt this could be a comparable vehicle to the Lexus. He wanted to ensure he had negotiated the best price for a quality vehicle. As it turns out, the price on the BMW came back much higher, and they could not deliver a vehicle before Christmas. Sure, he thought he was a top notch negotiator, little did he know the power behind my belief and targeted visualization. Shh... don't tell him... I still want him to believe it was his articulate research and strong negotiation skills that led to the purchase of the Lexus. I have a wonderful husband and family, and they usually play a large part in helping me reach my goals, but this also really solidified for me the power that an emotional attachment can bring to achieving any goal.

As I said, this goal was on my vision board for five years. You too may have some goals that take a great deal of time to accomplish, but eventually they will happen if you tap into the power that this process can bring. I encourage you to create a unique and individual vision board that represents what you want from your life and to review it daily to enhance the power of your intentions.

Action

Today is the day to start creating your own vision board. Return to your Top 6 Goals, Master List of Goals, and even your Be, Do and Have Lists. Look at what you wrote and collect pictures that relate to those goals. While you are scanning through magazines or print material, pay close attention to words, colors

---

or diagrams that connect with you. Don't think too long about whether you should have them on your board or not. If your eye is drawn to it, grab it and save it. Just focus on gathering a collection of visuals for your board. Once you start placing them on the board, only then will you decide what to keep and what to toss. For now, simply collect pictures with the intention of creating a collection of visuals that evoke a pleasant emotion and you enjoy looking at.

Daily Reflection

Before going to bed, review your gratitude list and reflect on the day's accomplishments. Look for the good in what you did today and reflect on the excitement of bringing your goals to life with a vision board. Embrace this excitement and move forward in your journey. Tomorrow is a new day, filled with new opportunities. As you close your eyes, picture the amazing day you will have tomorrow.

DAY 25
EXPLORE DIFFERENT TYPES OF VISION BOARDS

Begin Each

Day with

Gratitude

In your companion Next Level Living Workbook, record...

10 things I am grateful for today...

Dream lofty dreams, and as you dream, so you shall become. Your vision is the promise of what you shall one day be; your ideal is the prophecy of what you shall at last unveil.

-James Allen

◆ *Next Level Lesson* ◆
Different Types of Vision Boards

I have seen the power of vision boards over and over again, in my own life and in the lives of others. My friend Lisa, a registered nurse and fellow entrepreneur, shared with me her own experience in creating a vision board.

"For a few months before I actually created my vision board, I had experienced betrayal, both personal and

professional, that impacted me very deeply. As a result of the blow to my business, I had to look at the possibility of going back to the hospital setting to work as a staff nurse again, which I was not thrilled about at all because I had been in that environment for 20 years and did not want to go back. However, I knew financially it might be the only way to survive.

So I was in a very, very dark place, and I knew I had to work my way out of it. One Friday night in January at my office, I was done with clients and had brought everything to my office; all the magazines I had been serendipitously accumulating, my poster board, glue sticks, scissors, etc. I locked myself in my office and worked on it until I had completed my vision board. And I have to say, it literally transformed me – and quickly.

In February, I was talking to a friend of mine who had just opened a new pharmacy with her husband. I happened to mention to her husband that I was looking for a part-time or per diem nursing position. Ironically, they'd already discussed the possibility of hiring me at the pharmacy, because of my specific background. So this conversation was occurring and of course, I had just put on my vision board - to find a perfect job. Find was one word, Perfect was another, and J-O-B were separate. We met again the next week and they offered me a position. I found my perfect job! It has launched me into opportunities that I never would have dreamed of actually happening.

The moral of my story is: "Put your attention and your complete 100% intention and commitment to literally putting your vision on paper - seeing it, identifying it and taking ownership of it."

When we create vision boards in my Vision Board Workshops, we use an actual piece of poster board. We spend time finding and cutting out pictures from magazines that show the kind of life we want. Upon completion, each person displays their vision board in a prominent location in their home or office. You can however, develop this same type of idea in a notebook or three ring binder using heavy bond paper to hold your pictures. My friend and publisher, Dee, uses a spiral notebook and at the top of each page states her goal and a positive affirmation connected to that goal, such as "I am so happy and grateful that our family had a tremendous time on our cruise to Jamaica." Then she will put pictures of that cruise or the boat on the rest of the page. She also dates when she begins working toward each goal, so she can measure how long it takes her to achieve it. At the beginning of each day, she reviews this notebook to set the course of her day with intention and focus.

I have also seen people who do vision boards on the computer. This is also fine, but you must be sure that it is placed somewhere you will see every day, like as a desktop background or screensaver for instance.

Not only is a vision board effective, it's also fun! It gives you a place to allow your goals to develop into a concrete vision. So instead of having to imagine a tropical beach, you have a photo of one right in front of you that instantly takes your mind to that place.

There are several types of vision boards. Although these are by no means the only ones, here are the most common types I have found. You may start with one and then use another when the situation warrants.

Vision Board Types

1. **Business** – Focuses specifically on your vision for your business or work related area of your life and allows you to go in-depth into the many areas of business that you want to address.

2. **Whole Life** – Encompasses all the various facets of life. It can be split into sections, with one area designated for each facet, or you can combine them all and spread your images randomly on your board.

3. **Specific** – Focuses on just one of the eight facets we discussed earlier. Or you can focus on one specific goal, event or milestone, such as a wedding, running a marathon, or building a bigger savings account.

4. **Open and Allowing** – This vision board is for you, if you:

   a. Are not sure what you want.

   b. Have a vision of what you want, but are uncertain about it in some way.

   c. Know you want change but don't know how it is possible.

To create an Open and Allowing board, go through magazines, gather photos and collect images that make you feel good or that just make you smile. Don't ask "why," or second guess yourself, just enjoy the process.

The next step is to put the pictures on your board. As you do so, ask yourself what this image means to you. If you don't get an answer but still love the image, then put it on your board anyway. The answer will come to you when the time is right. This board might be just what you need because it doesn't have any specific planning involved. It operates from deep within by following your intuition. This kind of board can be a powerful guide for you.

5. **Annual** – This board includes your top goals for the year. Generally this board's images and goals are designed to be completed in a specific timeframe, usually by year's end.

6. **Transitional** – This board is for someone who has experienced grief, sadness, or major life change. You may have a difficult time completing the board in one sitting. That is fine. The point of the board is to help you get started in your transition and capture your thoughts and feelings about it. Transition in life is not easy, but this type of board gives you a place to capture the reality of where you are and where you want to go from here. It can be extremely uplifting!

Creating your own vision board does take a little time and planning, but it gives you a whole new perspective on your goals and dreams. As you capture your future in pictures, starting with just one picture if you choose, you are able to get really clear about your goals and even begin to imagine new ways to reach them.

People who have attended our Vision Board Workshops were in awe at how many things on their boards showed up in their lives. Jeana created her vision board dreaming of being engaged to her boyfriend Sammy, having the financial resources to buy Sammy the dog he has always wanted, and getting her college degree. I am thrilled to announce that we attended Jeana and Sammy's wedding a few weeks ago. Jeana graduated just before the wedding, and one of their wedding pictures included not one dog but two. Numerous stories like this have played out from people creating their own vision boards:

◆ Paige is driving the car of her dreams.

◆ Louisa and John are living in Atlanta, Georgia.

◆ Lisa found not just the perfect job but also now has a home on Lake Almanor.

◆ Jenifer has her own FM radio show.

And the book you are reading…yes you guessed it, it was on my vision board.

Keeping the Vision Fresh

Think of a time when a beautiful painting in the store caught your eye. From the various colors, aspects and emotions it stirred within you as you admired it - you just had to have it. So you purchased the painting, took it home and proudly displayed it on your wall. For the first few months, whenever you walked by it, you remained in awe of its beauty.

After some time passed, however, the same painting seemed to lose its allure. Suddenly it blended in unremarkably with its surroundings, and you stopped admiring it the way you did back in the beginning.

The same will hold true for your vision board, if you keep it one place for an extended period of time. This is why I encourage you to move your vision board around after a couple of months, especially if you find you are not taking time to look at it daily with fresh, eager eyes. Simply shifting the location of anything creates a sense of newness. It refreshes the environment, and you notice it differently. The key is that you are aware on a daily basis of your goals, your dreams and your vision. Be creative, move it around every few days, weeks or months. You will find yourself gazing at your vision board more often each time it finds a new place in your home.

Action

Now choose the type of vision board or vision book you would like to create.

Continue to collect the remaining materials needed:

◆ more magazines

◆ scissors

◆ glue stick

◆ poster board or heavy bond paper

◆ hole punch if you are making a vision book

Set aside time over the next few days to work on this project. This is a fun process that will have exciting results. You might want to recruit a buddy or two to do this exercise with you.

Daily Reflection

Before going to bed, review your gratitude list and reflect on what you accomplished today. See how your vision of life at the next level is steadily becoming a reality. Embrace what is and move forward to what will soon be. Tomorrow is a new day, filled with new opportunities. As you close your eyes, picture the amazing day you will have tomorrow.

DAY 26
KEEP PRESSING ON

Begin Each

Day with

Gratitude

In your companion Next Level Living Workbook, record...

10 courageous things about myself I am grateful for today...

As you write today's gratitude list, I want you to think of all the things about yourself that make you a super hero in your own life. This is the time to remind yourself that you are strong, you are brave, and you CAN do it!

◆ *Next Level Lesson* ◆
Keep Pressing On

A famous mountain climbing resort in the Swiss Alps caters to businesses that encourage their employees to hike up the mountain trails together. The goal is to build camaraderie and to teach teamwork. Although it is about an eight hour trek to the summit, anyone in reasonably good shape can ascend to the top.

In the morning, the hikers gather at the base of the mountain for a pep talk before starting the climb. Usually the group is so excited, they can hardly wait to head up the slopes, have a group picture taken, and celebrate the excitement of the journey they are on.

They hike for several hours before taking a break. About halfway up the mountain stands a quaint alpine restaurant. About noon, the weary hikers trudge into the restaurant, peel off their hiking gear, and plop down by the fireplace to have a cup of coffee or hot chocolate and eat their lunch. With the mountain as their backdrop, the hikers savor the warm, cozy, picturesque setting.

Interestingly, after they are full and comfortable, fewer than half the hikers choose to continue climbing to the top of the mountain. It isn't because they aren't able; it isn't because the climb suddenly appears too difficult. Their reluctance to continue is simply because they are satisfied with where they are. They've lost their drive to excel, to explore a new horizon, and to experience vistas they'd never previously imagined possible. They have tasted a bit of success, and they think it is good enough.

Many times, we approach life a lot like those full and comfortable hikers sitting in the restaurant enjoying the view. We have a goal to break a bad habit, to lose some weight, or to pay off our credit cards. At first, we're so excited. We're fired up and we go after it! The first leg of the climb up the mountain is powered by enthusiasm for our new goal. But over time, we get lazy and complacent. Maybe we see a little improvement, but then we get comfortable right where we are. This might not be a bad place, but we know it's not where we're supposed to be. Like those hikers sitting in that quaint restaurant, we are still perfectly capable of craning our necks and looking up the mountain. We're not stretching our faith or our potential and we know it. Maybe you own a business, and you've experienced a bit of success. Lately, however, you've been coasting. Or maybe you set out to lose 20 pounds, you lose 10, and feel like all is good and you get complacent. Don't stop halfway just because it's easy! Instead, remember what it is that you really, really want. Put out the effort and go the whole way... to the top of the mountain.

Action

Step out of your comfort zone today! Keep pursuing and keep believing. It doesn't take any more effort to believe and stay filled with hope and faith than it does to develop a negative and defeated attitude. Get up every day and say, "This is going to be a great day! I believe my dreams are coming to pass. There are great things in store for me and everyone around me." When you have that kind of attitude, you are releasing God's goodness. But it doesn't come easily.

People who see their dreams come to pass are people who have resolve and backbone. They are the ones who refuse to settle for the little victories along the way and see themselves at the finish line, instead pushing on toward the ultimate goal. No one wants to be mediocre. You are made for so much more. Realize that what your mind focuses on, it can achieve. It is up to you. Pay attention only to those silent whispers within that say "You can do it!"

As you are spending a few days working on your vision board, now is a great time to go back and review the work you have done up to this point. Remember where you are heading and why you are heading there. Spend a few minutes today reading through your Top 6 Goals and then continue working on your vision board until it is complete.

Daily Reflection

Before going to bed, review your list of courageous things about yourself that you are grateful for and reflect on the day's accomplishments. Look for the strength in what you did today. Celebrate it and move forward in your journey. Tomorrow is a new day, filled with new opportunities to succeed. As you close your eyes, picture the amazing day you will have tomorrow, leaping tall buildings in a single bound!

DAY 27
BE PERSISTENTLY PERSEVERANT

Begin Each Day with Gratitude

In your companion Next Level Living Workbook, record...

10 things I am grateful for today...

Ambition is the path to success, persistence is the vehicle you arrive in
                                        -William Eardley IV

◆ *Next Level Lesson* ◆
Persistence

Persistence means to endure, especially in the face of opposition. When persistence is "super sized," it is often referred to as perseverance, which means steady persistence in spite of even larger obstacles. So in a sense, perseverance is the next "level" above persistence. This doesn't make one more important than the other, just like when you move from one level to the next in life. Instead it is a reminder that value can be found in each quality.

It's easy to forget how persistent and perseverant we are by nature. The chaos and challenges of daily life can make us doubt ourselves. It can mask the inner strength that lies just below the surface. Sometimes we have to go back in time to remember a moment or incident that showed our true persistent colors. I did this recently for my daughter Brittany, reminding her of a time in her life when she displayed remarkable perseverance.

We had just moved from Canada to the U.S. and the kids were due to start school in a few days. Brittany was 14 at the time and my youngest daughter Paige was 10. Just days after we arrived, when we were still busy getting the house organized and settling in, there was a neighborhood block party.

"Can we go Mom, can we go Mom, can we go Mom, please?" the girls pleaded.

I told them yes, and that Scot and I would be along shortly.

So there's Brittany, the new kid at the neighborhood block party. We didn't know anyone in the neighborhood, but that didn't stop her from quickly making friends. Challenged to a scooter race by the boys in the neighborhood and being her equally adventurous father's daughter, Brittany eagerly accepted. During the race, mishap struck, slamming her mouth into the handle bars of the scooter. It was just a few days before her first day of school at a new school in a new country, and Brittany's front tooth was cracked beyond salvage and had to be pulled immediately.

The neighborhood response was remarkable! People we were meeting for the first time sprang into action and came to Brittany's aid. One neighbor who worked for a dental office was able to reach the dentist on the phone, even on a Sunday afternoon. The dentist took her into his office the following morning and then referred her to an oral surgeon. Brittany had to be fitted for a false tooth, first a temporary one called a "flipper" because it flipped down into the place where the broken tooth had been and where the permanent one would later be implanted. Imagine, a teenage girl having to deal with dentures and Poly Grip! At the emotionally volatile age of 14, in the midst of all this physical and emotional trauma, Brittany was the absolute picture of calm, composure and grace. She had a positive attitude, trusting that everything was going to be okay.

My husband and I were in shock! How many other 14 year old girls would have been willing to even step out of the house, let alone start a new school? We guess that most would have experienced a mini nuclear meltdown and refused to do ANYTHING... let alone show their face in public! Where did such a high level of inner perseverance come from?

Brittany told us later that she felt surrounded by people she loved and trusted, and that somehow gave her the inner strength and courage to carry on with a smile – "flipper" and all. The oral surgeon was also impressed, telling us, "You have raised an unbelievable daughter," and Scot and I agreed as we are proud of her wonderful qualities. Brittany chose a positive attitude, courage and trust over panic and giving up.

As I recounted this memory to Brittany, I could see she was instantly reminded of her inner perseverance. That's the thing about the strongest, most positive qualities that you possess, like persistence for instance. Once these qualities implant themselves in your soul, they are there forever. It's up to you to remember this and tap into them, especially when life tests you to see what you're made of.

By definition, persistence is the ability to remain in an endeavor or action in spite of adverse conditions or occurrences. You have to ask yourself, "How many times can I be knocked down (or over the handlebars of a scooter, in my daughter's case) and still get up and keep going? What is my limit? When will I quit?"

Have you given yourself a timeline in which you will try to reach your goal, and if it doesn't work you plan to go back to what you were doing before? Have you given yourself a worst-case scenario that will excuse you from trying anymore? If so, then you are giving yourself a reason to fail. You are hedging your bets rather than giving it one-hundred percent.

I know of a bestselling writer, Jodi Thomas, who tells the story of her career:

"I was a school teacher, and my husband is also a school teacher. We struggled to make ends meet with two young boys. I had always wanted to write a novel, and so I decided to do it, hoping I could at least put some money away for the boys' college education. I finished my first book in about a year and sent it out to every publisher in New York. Just as quickly, they sent it right back. The rejections were harsh, and one even included a two page single-spaced letter from a leading editor about how bad it really was.

It hurt terribly. Many times when I was depressed, I would go out to Llano Cemetery and sit for a while. It was calm and serene and gave me space to think. On one particular day, I was walking among the beautiful landscape and happened to see a large granite fruit bowl in the distance. I walked over and saw this bowl was surrounded by benches, so I sat for a while and cried my eyes out, certain that every dream I had of being a real author had been washed away. Finally, I looked down and on the cement by my feet was the word "triumph."

I thought it strange that there would be a word in the cement and started looking around the bowl of fruit. Each side of the bowl had a different word making up a single sentence. That sentence was "Triumph Comes Through Perseverance." I decided right then that those publishers in New York may never like one word that I write, but I refuse to quit."

She sold her next book and now, more than thirty years later, has published more than thirty-eight novels and is a New York Times best-selling author.

This is a good illustration of the fact that sometimes it can be difficult to pick a stopping point before you even start. You can't say, "I will try this for a year, and then I'll let myself give up." You have to give it everything you have and determine in your own mind that there is no going back.

Think about the vision you wrote down for your life in 5, 10 and 20 years on Day 16. Is it to provide a better life for your children or maybe give yourself time and financial freedom? Many of you have probably seen or heard stories about people who survive incredible hardships from accidents to days or weeks stranded on the open ocean. How do they do it? What separates them from the normal person that would most likely not survive in such a situation? The answer is that most of them have a very strong will to live. They have a strong purpose and a vision that they will overcome every hardship.

While the stakes may not be life and death, they are your future and represent the life you want. When you come upon hard times or face seemingly insurmountable obstacles, focusing on your vision will get you through and set you on a path to success.

Action

What will persistence and perseverance look like for you once you finish reading Next Level Living? Make a decision now about how you will master the art of persistence and perseverance before hardship sets in, to ensure your success in achieving your dreams and goals. Describe what you will do and who you need around you to help you be persistent in reaching your goals.

Daily Reflection

Before going to bed, review your gratitude list and reflect on the day's accomplishments. Look for the good in what you did today. Embrace your ability to exercise persistence and perseverance and move forward toward your next level. Tomorrow is a new day, filled with new opportunities. As you close your eyes, picture the amazing day you will have tomorrow.

Jewels for
the Journey
Burn Your Lifeboat

I heard a story once about a general who sent his army across the sea to an island to do battle. When they landed, the general and his lieutenant climbed the hill and realized that the opposing forces were many times greater than their army. The lieutenant asked the general what they should do, expecting him to say, "Retreat." Instead the general said, "Burn the lifeboats."

In your own life, you must be determined to "burn your lifeboats." If you do not give yourself the opportunity to quit or even find a way to remove any safety nets you've put in place for yourself, then you will be forced to move forward.

In my own life, when I finally got started writing this book, I shared the news excitedly with others verbally and in writing. I cast the vision for the goal I had set. Along the way, I encountered several delays in completing the project. But because I had a deep desire to share this information with others, and I had already told many friends and family about it, I was fully committed to its completion. So regardless of the circumstances, I kept pressing forward.

With the amazing supportive and talented people around me, this book has finally come to fruition and I am grateful that I set this goal, cast the vision, and persevered. And while there might be things I would do differently next time, I didn't quit on this one – I did burn the lifeboat and pressed forward.

You might feel you can't achieve something you have dreamed of or finish something you have started, but believe me, you can. Press forward and consider what it will mean for you to "burn the lifeboat."

DAY 28
GAIN SATISFACTION

Begin Each Day with Gratitude

In your companion Next Level Living Workbook, record…

10 things I am grateful for in this moment…

This moment is the only one that exists right now. When writing today's gratitude list, persuade your mind not to jump backward or forward in time, instead focus only on what you are feeling gratitude for right now.

◆ *Next Level Lesson* ◆
Satisfaction

As you focus on your affirmations, goals, and vision board, you will soon begin to reach the goals you set, and then you will start setting new goals and striving toward them. If this is your process, you may wonder at what point do you take a deep breath and proclaim, "I've arrived!" This is different for every individual. I can tell you that I certainly haven't gotten there yet.

Where is "there" anyway? Levels of living have no end. I am still growing and learning more each day. My goals change over time and that's okay. Life is about the journey. Success is not some magical destination that you will someday arrive at. It is about enjoying the growth and good things that happen along the way.

The idea of enjoying each moment of the journey reminds me of a poem by Robert J. Hastings called, The Station.

THE STATION

By Robert J. Hastings

TUCKED AWAY in our subconscious minds is an idyllic vision. We see ourselves on a long, long trip that almost spans the continent. We're traveling by passenger train, and out the windows we drink in the passing scene of cars on nearby highways, of children waving at a crossing, of cattle grazing on a distant hillside, of smoke pouring from a power plant, of row upon row of corn and wheat, of flatlands and valleys, of mountains and rolling hillsides, of city skylines and village halls, of biting winter and blazing summer and cavorting spring and docile fall.

But uppermost in our minds is the final destination. On a certain day at a certain hour we will pull into the station. There will be bands playing and flags waving. And once we get there so many wonderful dreams will come true.

So many wishes will be fulfilled and so many pieces of our lives finally will be neatly fitted together like a completed jigsaw puzzle. How restlessly we pace the aisles, damming the minutes for loitering, waiting, waiting, waiting for the station.

However, sooner or later we must realize there is no one station, no one place to arrive at once and for all. The true joy of life is the trip. The station is only a dream. It constantly outdistances us.

When we get to the station "that will be it!" we cry. Translated it means, "When I'm 18 that will be it! When I buy a new 450 SL Mercedes Benz, that will be it! When I put the last kid through college that will be it! When I have paid off the mortgage that will be it! When I win a promotion that will be it! When I reach the age of retirement that will be it! I shall live happily ever after!"

Unfortunately, once we get "it," then "it" disappears. The station somehow hides itself at the end of an endless track.

"Relish the moment" is a good motto, especially when coupled with Psalm 118:24: "This is the day which the Lord hath made, we will rejoice and be glad in it." It isn't the burdens of today that drive men mad. Rather, it is regret over yesterday or fear of tomorrow. Regret and fear are twin thieves who would rob us of today.

So, stop pacing the aisles and counting the miles. Instead, climb more mountains, eat more ice cream, go barefoot more often, swim more rivers, watch more sunsets, laugh more and cry less. Life must be lived as we go along. The station will come soon enough.

Action

You have journeyed through the past 28 days working on discovering, documenting and doing what you set out to do. You bought this book with the intention of taking your life to the next level. Sit back for a moment and enjoy your success and the progress you've made so far. You might not realize how much progress you've actually made until you look down that staircase back at the level where you started. Quite a lot of stairs aren't they? Congratulate yourself on your progress – you deserve it!

What three things have you learned about yourself from going through the process up to this day? What has been difficult? Why was it difficult? What has been beneficial? Why was it beneficial? What has been motivating? Why was it motivating?

Daily Reflection

Before going to bed, review your gratitude list and reflect on the day's accomplishments. Look for the good in what you did today and the progress you've made so far. Embrace what you are feeling in this moment before moving forward in your journey. Tomorrow is a new day, filled with new opportunities. As you close your eyes, picture the amazing day you will have tomorrow.

DAY 29
REACH FOR YOUR ROPE OF HOPE

Begin Each

Day with

Gratitude

In your companion Next Level Living Workbook, record...

10 things I am grateful for today...

Here is the basic rule for winning success... Success depends on the support of other people. The only hurdle between you and what you want to be is the support of other people.

-David Joseph Schwartz

◆ *Next Level Lesson* ◆
Rope of Hope

No matter what is going on in your life, you need something to hold onto. This can be one of your support beams, a friend, spouse, mentor, family member or your higher power. It is someone who can toss you an emotional life preserver when things look dark and dim. A Rope of Hope is more than just hope for the future, but instead it promotes real expectation that those things we desire will come to pass. Hope is a feeling that things will be okay. Sometimes it is difficult to reconnect with this type of hope when things are not going well.

I can think of several times in my own life when I experienced the death or illness of a loved one, lost a close relationship, or had an emotional upset that threatened to overwhelm me. It was at those times that I felt the need to reconnect with my own Rope of Hope which for me is my faith. I wanted to get back in touch with a power bigger than myself, that would once again help me feel that things were going to work out and be okay.

For you it may be reconnecting with old friends or family or getting back to core values. It can be anything that helps to lessen the fear and stress associated with the circumstance and allows you the opportunity to step back and see the bigger picture. Hope is that little spark that convinces you to keep going, because you have a chance to work things out. And of course, hope is a key component to happiness.

Action

Who or what would you consider to be your Rope(s) of Hope? If you don't have one, who/what are some options you could consider?

Daily Reflection

Before going to bed, review your gratitude list and reflect on the day's accomplishments. As we move into the last leg of your journey, look for examples of how the people who love you have been supporting you the whole time. See the good in what you did today. Embrace it and move forward. Tomorrow is a new day, filled with new opportunities. As you close your eyes, picture the amazing day you will have tomorrow.

JEWELS FOR
THE JOURNEY
YOUR RAINBOW RING

Let's talk for a minute about those days where you feel like the rain is pouring down, and you feel less than motivated, harsh words are directed at you, or sadness overwhelms you.

In all probability, you might feel less than spectacular and wonder if you actually are deserving of this treatment. The thought flashes across your mind that maybe they're right – you are worthless and don't deserve great things. But you DO deserve great things!

In addition to your Ropes of Hope we just discussed, a powerful tool for you to pull out in these situations is a Rainbow Ring or Rainbow File.

A Rainbow Ring is a ring on which you assemble a collection of positive remarks written about you. These are visual reminders that you have done a great job, touched someone's heart by your actions, or inspired someone by your words.

Think of how you feel when you receive a nice card, email or voicemail complimenting you for a job well done or acknowledgement of your caring attitude.

Reading or hearing those meaningful words describing something you did extremely well stimulates emotions. Emotions then affect motivation.

How to gather material for your Rainbow Ring or Rainbow File:

◆ Save any emails, cards, letters, or notes that speak positive words about YOU.

◆ Or, when someone says something about you that makes you feel INCREDIBLE, jot it down on a 3X5 card and include it in your Rainbow collection.

◆ Gather pictures of you feeling HAPPY, POWERFUL, APPRECIATED, LOVED.

◆ Place all the things you gathered into a file or hole punch each of them and string them on a lose leaf ring.

Then, on those days when you feel like the sun isn't shining down on you, pull out your Rainbow Ring/File, read, reread and look at the collection of positive remarks written about you. Go back in time and remember how you felt when you first received those words. Deeply connect with that initial emotion you felt and allow it to move you away from the clouds into a day of beautiful rainbows. The sun is shining down on you because you are beautiful inside and worthy of great things.

REVIEW

Congratulations you have accomplished 29 days of Next Level Living!

In this part of your journey you have...

◆ Discovered why Affirmations are important.

◆ Learned the 6 steps to creating valuable Affirmations.

◆ Documented Affirmations corresponding to your Top 6 Goals List.

◆ Discovered the 6 different types of Vision Boards.

◆ Chosen the best type of Vision Board for yourself and created it.

◆ Become clear on how to maintain persistence and determination to reach your goals.

◆ Identified Your Rope(s) of Hope.

◆ Created your Rainbow Ring

A special gift for you... To keep you going down the home stretch, I want to offer you a gift of a free coaching call with one of the certified coaches on my team. Give us a call and we can discuss what you have accomplished, ensure you are making the most of this whole process and help you get focused on your next steps as you complete the last few days of the book. Contact my office at info@McLeanInternational.com, let us know you are working through Next Level Living, and we will schedule your free session.

SECTION FOUR
CELEBRATE YOUR JOURNEY

Day 30 ◆ Complete the Circle with Celebration

Day 31 ◆ Discover the Difference Between Happiness and Joy

Day 32 ◆ Celebrate You

Review

Conclusion ◆ The Journey Continues

Appendix A ◆ Types of Support Beams

Appendix B ◆ My Be, Do, and Have Lists

Appendix C ◆ Affirmations

Appendix D ◆ Connector Affirmations

DAY 30
COMPLETE THE CIRCLE WITH CELEBRATION

Begin Each

Day with

Gratitude

In your companion Next Level Living Workbook, record...

10 things to celebrate that I am grateful for today...

> *The more you praise and celebrate your life,*
> *the more there is in life to celebrate.*
> *-Oprah Winfrey*

◆ *Next Level Lesson* ◆
Celebration Completes the Circle

The act of celebrating our accomplishments is very important to our continued success. It is a powerful tool that creates further momentum. And make no mistake, it sends an inspiring message to others, giving them permission to start celebrating their own accomplishments as well.

Have you ever held back on acknowledging your wins or even sharing your accomplishments with others because you didn't want to appear to be bragging or drawing undeserved attention to yourself?

Now is the time to acknowledge yourself and enjoy a little celebration. You don't have to be a "show off." It can be a subtle personal celebration or shared with family members or friends who sincerely take joy in your accomplishments.

Why Celebration is Important

Without taking the time to celebrate how we are showing up in the world, we starve our hearts of acknowledgement. Without pausing to celebrate, we continue to pile up things on our "to do" list, thinking we haven't done enough. This is exactly how many of us create that sense of perpetual busyness, with no deeper sense of meaning to our efforts. Celebration, on the other hand, allows us to stop and enjoy what we have accomplished. It gives us that sense that we have made progress. We are moving forward.

Action

Take some time to consider your own life. I am sure you can easily find numerous things to celebrate, just from this journey to your next level alone. Have fun, take a chance and think of the things you could celebrate that you have accomplished this past week, month, and six months. You've made it to the final section of Next Level Living. Doing your exercises and growing over the last 30 days calls for a fist pump or victory dance – doesn't it?

Daily Reflection

Before going to bed, review your gratitude list and reflect on your personal celebrations of the day. Acknowledge the good in what you did today, embrace it and move forward. You are closer to your next level than ever before! Tomorrow is a new day, filled with new opportunities. As you close your eyes, picture the

DAY 31
THE DIFFERENCE
BETWEEN HAPPINESS AND JOY

In your companion Next Level Living Workbook, record…

10 reasons to be happy today…

Happiness is like a thermometer that changes based on the environment around it. Joy, on the other hand is a thermostat that we can learn to set and it will affect the environment around it.

-Source Unknown

◆ *Next Level Lesson* ◆
The difference between Happiness and Joy

Happiness is something that you find in the moment. You can be happy because you've just had a great laughing spurt with a friend or because you did something good or your kids did something that's really awesome. Happiness is determined by your circumstances. Therefore, happiness is an emotion usually uncovered in the moment. When the circumstances are good and going our way, we feel happy. On the other hand, when things break, when we do not get what we want or we are disappointed, we lose our happiness and feel sad.

Joy on the other hand is entirely different. Joy is an attitude of the heart. It comes from within and is a daily choice you make. Joy runs deep. It is not necessarily based on something positive happening in one particular moment. I've heard some express a belief that joy is genetic, something we are born with embedded in our soul, while happiness is a temporary and often fleeting state of mind. You do find people who are just naturally joyful, who exude the attitude that life is generally pretty good. Children seem to have natural joy, cheer and excitement. They have an enchanted air about them. Some would call this innocence, because they haven't yet tasted the pains of life, but this reflects a certain natural state that we all have within us. As we get older, however, we forget to dip into our "bowl of joy" more and more. Connecting (and continually reconnecting) with your joy can provide a sense of peace and comfort even in the midst of a storm.

Imagine if you bump your toe, are you happy about it? Probably not. But can you maintain joy? Absolutely. It goes back to choosing not to focus on the bumped toe, but keeping your focus on the joy of having a toe to bump! People who choose to live their lives with joy have lots of enthusiasm to do wonderful things and often have a big impact on the world. Joy is an important component of living a life to the fullest. So I encourage you to choose to be joyful about your life whatever the circumstances you find yourself in.

Action

Write down specific things that make you happy. If you need some suggestions, here are a few of mine:

◆ Laughing with my brothers and sisters

◆ Checking things off my "to do list"

◆ Cuddling with my daughters

◆ Listening to some of my favorite songs and dancing

◆ Traveling with my husband

◆ Planning a dinner

◆ Getting positive feedback from clients or from a speaking engagement

◆ Drinking a cup of Tim Horton's coffee with one of my dearest friends

◆ Witnessing "ah-ha moments" of family, friends and clients

◆ Harnessing the power of "I can do it"

◆ Standing on the balcony of my friend's cottage, drinking a cup of coffee enjoying the beautiful view of the lake

◆ Taking a nap on a cold, rainy day

◆ Hearing a great message at church

◆ Getting a pedicure

I could have filled up pages of specific things that bring me happiness. I'll bet you can too. So think about all the things in this world that make you happy. It could be small things, big things, or all the other things in between.

Now, write down specific ways you connect with Joy in your life. If you need some suggestions, here are a few of mine:

◆ Having quiet time in the morning to reflect and prepare for the day ahead

◆ Embracing gratitude (through my gratitude list) for the things and people around me

◆ Relaxing on the beach or on my friend's boat on a beautiful sunny day

◆ Admiring the rich fall colors

◆ Enjoying an amazing blue sky from a snow covered mountain top while skiing

◆ Being a member of the Brigley family

◆ Experiencing motherhood

Write out three things that could (or do) connect you with Joy in your life. Feel free to include more if you want.

Daily Reflection

Before going to bed, review your gratitude list and reflect on the day's accomplishments. Look for the happiness and joy you found throughout the day. Embrace this and move forward in your journey to the next level. Tomorrow is a new day, filled with new opportunities. As you close your eyes, picture the amazing day you will have tomorrow.

DAY 32
CELEBRATE YOU

Begin Each Day with Gratitude

In your companion Next Level Living Workbook, record...

10 things I am grateful for today...

The journey is the reward.

-Chinese Proverb

◆ *Next Level Lesson* ◆
Celebrating You

I have heard many people comment that "they don't celebrate birthdays anymore." And I say hooey to that! When I turned 50, I claimed the entire year to celebrate. I would say, "I am 50, fabulous and having fun!" I purposely shared this with people, and before I knew it others were fully engaged in my celebration. And you guessed it, they had fun as well.

From traveling to Miami with my Ya Ya girlfriends, to a surprise visit from my girlfriends from Canada, to many other moments, parties, acknowledgements from my husband and my daughters and the many students and friends that came to our house that year – it was a fabulous time of celebration. What happiness it brought not just to me, but to others as well. It was as though my inviting them to celebrate with me gave them each their own birthday blessing. I have since passed this message on to many friends, encouraging them to embrace and enjoy their birthday year as well.

I encourage you to Celebrate, Celebrate, Celebrate every opportunity you can, not only because you deserve it, but also because it can serve as inspiration for others to follow in your footsteps, honoring their own accomplishments along the way.

Action

Make a list of how you would like to celebrate and with whom (if anyone) you will do this celebrating. Get it on your calendar and don't let the busyness of life take over.

Stand strong at this new level you have achieved. You deserve the acknowledgement, the recognition, and the celebration. You have earned it for pushing forward, exploring, testing, writing, thinking and charting your roadmap to success. And all along you have been striving to reach a higher level in your life. Embrace it and enjoy it!

Daily Reflection

Before going to bed, review all your gratitude lists from your journey and reflect on all the incredible accomplishments of your Next Level Living journey. Look for the positive in what you did today and for the past 32 days. Embrace it ALL and continue moving forward! Tomorrow is a new day, filled with new opportunities. As always, as you close your eyes, picture the amazing day you will have tomorrow and all the days beyond. The journey never ends and your available levels are infinite!

Review

Celebration is critical!

In these final days of our journey together you have...

◆ Learned why celebration is important.

◆ Started your own list of things you can celebrate.

◆ Discovered the difference between Happiness and Joy.

◆ Listed things that make you happy and listed things that connect you to joy.

◆ Documented how, when and with whom you will celebrate.

CONCLUSION
THE JOURNEY CONTINUES...

If you saw where I came from, you would know how amazing this journey has truly been for me. I grew up on a farm in Canada; my hometown had only 1,500 residents (that's including cats and dogs). In a farm family of six kids, chores were plentiful and time and money were not. I was well aware that the kids I went to school with were able to experience life luxuries that were not available to me. For instance, I always wanted to take dance lessons, but that was simply not a possibility, nor were vacations or big presents. That was simply the reality of that particular level of my journey.

However, where we lacked leisure time and money, we made up in closeness as a family. I continue to honor my parents today for providing that inner core of what family truly means and cherish the wonderful relationships I have with my brothers and sisters. And that entire small town remains a part of that core. If I fly in and need a place to stay, a hot meal, or even a horse to borrow, people show up; family members come out of the woodwork and eagerly give of themselves without a second thought. For me, learning what family and community really means was the jewel that I gained from that level of my journey, and I will treasure it forever.

Now, I live in a different country on a completely different level with many blessings bestowed on myself and my family. But the inner core, the true meaning of family, has moved with me from level to level, during hard times and good. That's the thing... The most important things travel with you and continue to increase; you never have to worry about accidentally leaving them behind as your continue your journey.

From farm girl, to cancer survivor, to international speaker, author and world traveler...Most people who meet me don't guess that life has thrown me some challenging curve balls on various levels along the way. I often wonder how I made it through.

Nevertheless, I found a way to slowly move forward, push through the storm and come out into the sunshine.

Every once in a while, the ugly demons of nasty negative "self-talk" creep back into my mind and attempt to take root like a stubborn weed. With frustration I wonder WHY does this happen when I know better? I push back and I am reminded of Vivian Greene who said "Life is not about waiting for storms to pass... it's about learning how to dance in the rain!" I dance and I dance as often as I can. Join me in the dance to the next level. If a farm girl from the prairies of Alberta, Canada can create positive change in her life and push through to her next level, you can too!

Once you change the course of your own life, it ripples out like circles in a pond touching untold numbers of lives for the better or the worse, depending on the ripples you are sending out. I encourage you to continue your Next Level Living journey and make your own positive ripples in life. You will be leaving those you love the tremendous gift of hope – the hope that their lives can be as full and joyful as your own.

Although we are wrapping up Next Level Living, from here your journey does not end but really just begins. You have the opportunity to put into action all you have learned and to truly create the life of your dreams.

For me (and my family) the Next Level Living process is one we go through once a year. Almost always there are major "ah-ha moments." As you wrap up your 32 days, be sure to share your "ah-ha" moments with others and also record them for yourself. And know my hope and prayer for you is that this has helped you reach a new level and feel better than ever. I look forward to seeing you on the Next Level (www.nextlevellivingbook.com). Until then, keep your flashlight on, your roadmap in hand and always search for that next staircase upward.

With warmth, gratitude and encouragement,

Linda

APPENDIX A

TYPES OF SUPPORT BEAMS

Along life's journey, there are many different challenges you will have to deal with. You need to recognize and honor the types of "support beams" you have established ahead of time. They are ways of supporting you as you experience life's challenges. Here are some categories of "support beams" that I recommend.

Read: phrases, quotes, verses, novels, magazines, poetry

Environment: the inspiration of your office, favorite chair, relaxing room, outdoors

Visual Tools: paintings, pictures, affirmation cards, scenery, Vision Board/Book, motivational DVD's

Tactile: a soft blanket, sand between your toes, wind upon your face, the warmth of fire

Smell: pine trees, fresh flowers, fresh cut grass

Touch: massage, hugs, pedicures

Physical: exercise, tennis, golf, running

People: family, friends, neighbors, a mentor, coach, teacher

Rest: meditation, prayer, sleep, vacation

Sounds: music, ocean waves, motivational CD's

APPENDIX B

MY BE, DO, AND HAVE LISTS

Who I want to BE (or become) before I leave this earth.

A great mother who is a good role model in all different areas of life

A great wife who is also a friend and partner to my husband

A good golfer scoring on average 100 for 18 holes

A confident, skier with good technique successfully skiing blacks & double blacks

An author, with four books ranked as best sellers

A contributing community member

A fun, energetic, healthy Grandmother

Things I want to DO before I leave this earth.

Take Cooking Classes

Travel to many countries (I have created a separate list of countries)

Take my daughters on a tour of the wine country in Napa/ Sonoma

Go white water rafting with family/friends

Be at the birth of my grandchild/grandchildren

Write a book

Hike at Yosemite National Park

Things I want to HAVE before I leave this earth.

Princess cut, diamond earrings – total 1 carat

Happy memorable moments with family and friends

Financial security in retirement representing $_____ per year (I have filled in my own number)

Annual vacations with family and friends

Home (2-3 bedroom) in ski area – no outside maintenance

Matching – husband/wife – awesome watches

Bernard Passman, "Past, Present and Future" Ring

Lakefront Cottage/Cabin (3-4 bedroom) with a spectacular view and awesome beach area

APPENDIX C
AFFIRMATIONS

I Love Myself, therefore....

◆ I am feeling the power of a healthy body and mind.

◆ I am so happy now that money comes to me in increasing quantities, through multiple sources on a continuous basis.

◆ I am celebrating the happy relationships I have with my family, friends and business associates.

◆ I am growing in my spiritual journey.

◆ I am participating in a daily quiet time reflecting, praying and visualizing.

◆ I am feeling the exhilaration of being fit, tone and weighing ___ lbs.

◆ I am delighted that I look younger than ___ yrs.

◆ I am proud that I am eating fruits, vegetables, carbs and protein in balance.

◆ I am delighted my home is completely decorated and renovated to my desire.

◆ I am effectively listening to what others have to say with genuine interest and respect.

◆ I am feeling proud that I stay focused and on task.

◆ I am actively embracing the opportunities that come with change.

◆ I am enough for all that I desire.

◆ I am ecstatic that I am giving to others monetarily.

◆ I am choosing to live a vibrant and healthy life.

◆ I am so happy now that I am feeling fit by exercising 3 times per week.

◆ I am feeling so peaceful when I spend time each day meditating.

◆ I am filled with quality ideas and the ability to bring them into action.

◆ I am the person who makes my dreams come true.

◆ I am experiencing joy traveling the world with family and friends.

APPENDIX D
CONNECTOR AFFIRMATIONS

Affirmations that help position your thinking and help you connect to certain emotions and mindsets.

I take the initiative to create my life the way I want it.

I deeply appreciate & accept myself just the way I am.

I am valuable as a person even when I make mistakes.

I listen to what others have to say with genuine interest & respect.

I accept my divine right to personal power & I express that power in everything I do.

I actively embrace the opportunities that come with change.

My body is a perfect mirror of divine perfection.

I am an open channel for love and healing.

I choose to live a vibrant and healthy life.

I am worth the money I receive.

CPSIA information can be obtained at www.ICGtesting.com
Printed in the USA
LVOW071339260212

270472LV00007B/51/P